In Other Woods

The Story of a Small School

In Other Woods

The Story of a Small School

Mary-Ann Ridgway

T

Troubador Publishing Ltd
Unit E2 Airfield Business Park
Harrison Road, Market Harborough
Leicestershire LE16 7UL
Tel: 0116 279 2299
Email: books@troubador.co.uk
Web: www.troubador.co.uk

ISBN 978 1 80514 320 8

British Library Cataloguing in Publication Data.
A catalogue record for this book is available from the British Library.

Printed and bound in Great Britain by 4edge Limited
Typeset in 11pt Garamond Pro by Troubador Publishing Ltd, Leicester, UK

To
the future of our children

Contents

The Redwood raven
Saw freedom reimagined
Every day anew[1]

1 'Inwoods from above' by Emma Sumpster (former staff and parent)

Introduction

Twenty-two years ago, on a beautiful autumn day, I followed six young children as they marched in celebratory style, holding candles and flowers, to our newly constructed barn classroom on the two acres of woodland glade that were our school. It was a turning point in my contributions to a growing education village, and I felt both nervous and excited. Having been an assistant, I was now assigned a group of children of my own. The responsibility felt immense.

Forty-four years ago, I was a child myself and instead of holding flowers, I held fear in my sweaty palms as I lined up for class. I obediently waited to be told what to do, then to be tested and subsequently diminished by my school-induced self-deprecating thoughts as I was forced to compare myself to others; learning was daunting.

We are a society that is destroying the earth, perpetuating poverty, and dividing people through patriotic thinking, oppression, corrupt relationships, and war. Is there another way of living on this planet? How is education contributing to this current state of affairs and what role can it hold for the future of humanity?

As I followed those joyful children with flowers in their hands, I asked myself, "How can I do things differently? Can I, along with my colleagues, the parents, and the numerous volunteers and individuals who pass through our inclusive place of learning, meet the children without imposing our conditioned ways? What approach would nurture young minds to remain alive and alert, and free of the destructive devices of fear, comparison, and evaluation, endemic to most educational settings?"

In Other Woods is the story of an offbeat primary school, which I began writing when my service to this place came to an end after over twenty years of committed involvement. What started as a reflective piece of personal work and a desire to capture some noteworthy stories, evolved into a deeper exploration of the intentions and life of a small school, that exposes what I have come to regard as essential and widely relevant concerns in education.

I make no claims to have found a solution to our troubled educational world, and this is not a book promoting specific methods. Rather, it opens a window into the raw reality and challenges of a daring and delicate educational endeavour, highlighting the connection between our relationship with each other and the critical state of the world.

"In oneself lies the whole world and if you know how to look and learn, the door is there and the key is in your hand. Nobody on earth can give you either the key or the door to open, except yourself."
J. Krishnamurti

The bluebell woods, den building and many memories on the walk including my first ever walk to school

· 1 ·

From Child to 'Educator'

I was born in Winchester, England, and raised the first
eight years of my life in London in the early seventies,
where I attended a Catholic school. I have memories of the
freedom my parents gave me to play uninterruptedly in the
neighbourhood with my friends and older sibling: on bikes
and skates, climbing walls, and exploring an old railway line
at the end of the street, while at the same time experiencing
the restrictive and controlling approach of some of the
nuns at school. I witnessed one nun pull down the pants
of a child in front of the whole class and spank her. Though
the punished girl was considered a rebellious, unfriendly
character at times, I was horrified by this act of aggression
and humiliation by an adult who was also preaching the
importance of 'goodness' and 'love'. This contradiction
struck me already at this young age and became more
apparent in subtle ways as I matured and continued my
educational journey.

My family left London for the 'good life' in Wales when I

was eight years old. We went from living in a terraced house in a large city to a 17th-century cottage on nine acres of land in the middle of the countryside. There, I experienced even more outdoor freedom and learnt to orientate myself on long walks alone and through visits by bike to friends in nearby villages. I learnt how to cut wood, build dens, put up swings in daring locations, look after hens, and skilfully climb trees. I learnt to put up with icy bed sheets in winter in a home with no central heating, and sit in the candlelit darkness when the 50p electricity meter ran out and there weren't the right coins to charge it up until the following day. One of my favourite games was playing 'school' with my two younger siblings.

Real school, however, was the local village Primary, where classes were relatively small. My fondest memories were of the art and craft lessons, the extra reading support I received from a caring 'special needs' teacher, and two special friends: a boy called Rawlins in a wheelchair who I often pushed around in the playground and who made me laugh, and a girl called Abigail from a large somewhat dysfunctional family with an alcoholic father. She was a feisty lass and the most caring and honest person I knew. One day, while queuing up to go for lunch, another friend tried to humiliate me by informing everyone that I had wet her bed during a sleepover the day before and that her mother had to burn the mattress. Abigail didn't hesitate for a second to speak up and inform everyone, in a matter of fact way, that she also wets the bed sometimes and that it didn't matter.

This other friend was the daughter of the school's music teacher. She lived in one of the largest detached posh houses in the village that I remember, with an immaculate interior that included a grand piano and thick-piled white carpets. On the other hand, Abigail lived in a small, terraced building with her seven brothers and parents, which often smelt of alcohol, chips, and urine. I learnt then that class, wealth, ability, or appearance had no bearing on any significant friendship or capacity to care.

Primary school life was relatively 'ok' until I encountered the headteacher, Mr Bond. In Year six, when I was ten, he became my class teacher. The thing I remember about this man was his capacity for intimidating looks. He had a way of staring us down until we were coerced into action or retreated into humiliation. I remember him asking all the children to stand behind their chairs while he demanded answers to multiplication questions to each of us, one by one; we could sit down once we had correctly answered. Mathematics not being my strong point, meant that on several occasions he put me on the spot for what seemed like an eternity as he silently stared me into a shameful piece of ignorance that all my classmates could take note of. Needless to say, the stress blocked the required cognitive work, and I was often the last to sit down. That class was held together by fear perpetuated by a passive-aggressive controlling adult.

On another occasion, after I had witnessed many similar distasteful approaches not just with me, I stood up for myself; the issue was my late arrival to school, which Mr Bond refused to accept my reasons for. That time, instead of allowing him to continue to ridicule me publicly without defence, I attempted to correct his nonfactual comments, which then prompted him to send me sharply to his office in disapproval. I waited there in apprehension, however, with enough time alone to feel and think about the injustice of his actions. When he arrived and tried to reprimand me for my outspokenness, I explained – with incredible lucidity that I didn't know I was capable of – how unkind his disrespectful manner was and how false his assumptions were. By the end of my sharing, he was flustered, apologetic, and tried to persuade me not to report his behaviour to my parents.

Reflecting now on that fearless and lucid moment of communication, I have noticed many children at a certain period in their growth have a way of expressing the gravity of a situation that is neither just an emotional outpouring nor a persuasive articulated argument, but a combination of feeling and thought working together. When emotions are not repressed, and the intellect has not become calculative, children can reveal important perceptions if we are open enough to hear them. However, overall, our upbringing and education emphasise improved intellect while discouraging emotions, though it is perhaps the integration of the two that is needed to grasp a broader and more in-depth understanding of life.

Secondary school was not a better experience in terms of teacher relationships and the environment. In fact, far worse: a school of two thousand children; class sizes up to forty; year groups with a notorious reputation for bad behaviour (I happened to be in one of them); more humiliation tactics from the teachers; and bullying from the students (though strangely that impacted me less). I remember the physics teacher using his extra long ruler to shock the students into action. He would slam it down on his desk at the front of the class, evaporating our giggles and banter in an instant and leaving behind a deathly silence of fear.

But what if fear also evaporates? As one can imagine by now, these atmospheres weren't very conducive to learning, and as a result, I often landed at the bottom of the class in terms of examination results, which led me to believe that I was not a strong candidate for academic achievements. One day I brought my physics textbook home to study in preparation for the upcoming end-of-term exam. I assumed this would be fruitless as I didn't feel I had understood very much – though I had somewhat enjoyed playing around with Bunsen burners, pinhole cameras, and electrical circuits. I presented the textbook to my father, who had a natural interest in the themes contained there (despite not having studied the subject much himself), and he went through the book carefully with me, from chapter to chapter, explaining what he could. We covered most of the term's curriculum presented at school in the space of a few hours. The experience was interesting and full of care; I wanted to learn from my father, and he wanted to 'teach' me. The outcome was that my exam results were considerably elevated from the usual and everyone looked at me in disbelief as the scores were unnecessarily read out in class.

Unresolved psychological fear is crippling and moulding. It conditions us to react in ways that don't make rational sense, often impacting our capacities to learn and our relationships with others. Opportunities to engage in life are reduced as we remain within the zone of what feels safe and comfortable. Most of us are a product of our fears, hurts, and insecurities which inevitably have a far-reaching and immensely significant impact on the world. Is there anything we can do to prevent schools from bringing fear into their environments as tactics to propel the young into actions of compliance? There may be less physical aggression in most schools nowadays, but there remains humiliation disguised as incentivising behaviour charts, public comparisons of ability, threats of reduced freedoms, and bribery disguised as pretty reward stickers. Is it possible to uproot those psychological fears and conditioning behaviour as part of the world's educational endeavours? Jiddu Krishnamurti seemed to think so.

J. Krishnamurti founded Brockwood Park School in 1969, an international residential secondary school. He was interested in psychological revolution, inquiry, human relationships, and radical change in society. He had no allegiance to any nationality, caste, religion, or philosophy and spent most of his life travelling the world, speaking to large and small groups, as well as individuals. In terms of education, Krishnamurti believed that it required a holistic outlook free from all prejudice, in which the educator is also being educated, and that a deep affection between people everywhere would resolve many problems, including the environmental challenges.

This brings me to the next critical phase of my education journey. My grandparents and my parents had been attending some of the yearly talks Krishnamurti gave each summer on the beautiful grounds of Brockwood Park School. I also came to these gatherings but spent most of the time either at the temporary creche provided for the occasion or in play with other children on the grounds around the big marquee that was set up to host many hundreds of attendees. It was only in the summer of 1984, at the age of fourteen, that I became curious and interested enough to attend one of the talks. It was a precious experience. Krishnamurti, somewhat frail at the age of eighty-nine, calmly sat on a modest podium so that everyone could see him. He would tuck his hands under his thighs, wait for calm to envelop the marquee, and then begin to address the public at a slow, attentive and precise pace. I remember him speaking about attention on this occasion while at the same time my being struck by the beauty of a tiny spider making a delicate journey along its invisible web between the two chairs in front of me. Krishnamurti's words were simple yet carried incredible depth and a sense of great urgency.

Once I had expressed my interest in this talk to my parents, it was only some weeks later that I was privileged to become a Brockwood Park student. The Director at the time, Dorothy Simmons, fast-tracked me through admissions so I missed the usual prospective week that would have been an opportunity to check out the place first. But I was not disappointed. Relative to my experiences so far of *schools*, this seemed like heaven. On a first-name basis, the adults were approachable, classes were small and only a little intimidating in that I couldn't hide anywhere.

To begin with, I was seriously shy, perhaps neurotically so, having been convinced by my previous educators that I didn't have much capacity to learn. My favourite activities were sports, walks, painting, drama and folk-dancing. I remember feeling both awkward and elated when my maths teacher held one of my hands and the physics teacher the other as we stepped the Israeli Manavu dance around the room in a circle with others. I particularly enjoyed playing basketball (though I would have been considered too short for such a sport in other schools), which was often a mixed team of girls, boys, students, teachers, all playing for fun and exercise rather than competition. This school was nothing like any place I had experienced, but it took many months to restore in me some level of confidence in learning. Krishnamurti passed away a year and a half later. His presence there was always unassuming and exuding great affection.

I was five years at Brockwood Park appreciating the non-competitive and non-conforming environment, the lack of emphasis on status and popularity, the community spirit towards looking after the place, and the ongoing attempts at inquiring into Krishnamurti's fundamental questions on life and learning. I was one of the very few fortunate students to have a full bursary for four years. With minimal funds available to me, the school let me stay during several holiday periods where I helped to repaint the rooms, clean, garden and assist in preparing meals. Brockwood was more than a school; it became my home, my family. But it was not a perfect place; there were concerning incidents and issues in my time there like most places. Already then I began to see that staff struggled in their relationships with each other; there were subtle power dynamics and questionable student expulsions.

No structure or strategy will provide the model answer towards a harmonious place. We can argue and experiment endlessly with decision-making and efficient systems (no doubt making some obvious or nuanced improvements), but as long as the *self* is at the forefront, pushing for its security and recognition, there will be breakdowns in relationships and an inability to work together to see *what* is right rather than *who* is right.

At the age of eighteen, I left Brockwood after having made some deep friendships and joined a travelling school with a group of nine others, none of whom I knew. This school aimed at having direct experience with people actively and passionately engaged in their field of interest. In Italy, we harvested grapes, made wine, built an outdoor kiln, and made pots and masks from our homemade clay. We spent six months in India between the north and south, engaging with children and teachers in schools, hiking to the source of the river Ganges, collecting rare orchids in a botanical sanctuary, living with traditional folk musicians and spending quiet days in pleasant retreat centres. There were many opportunities to dialogue, learn about the nature of relationships, and participate in workshops on art and theatre, including giving a street performance in Calcutta. These experiences were a welcome and needed change from the protective nest of Brockwood Park, where I had probably grown too comfortable. There was no possibility of forming cliques (we were only nine in the group!) or hiding from duties or shying away from one's responsibility to learn and engage with others. We witnessed suffering in India as well as the passion of individuals seeking ways to look after the planet (living and nonliving) with minimal personal gain and outside the context of any ideology.

While staying for some days at the Krishnamurti Retreat Centre in Uttarkashi, India, I read Krishnamurti's book, 'Education and the Significance of Life'. It was at this point that I became clear that education was my calling. Every word in that book resonated with my understanding of the issues children were facing and what schools needed to become. I returned to the UK rich with experience and with clarity and direction. Firstly, I trained in the Montessori approach to education for children up to age eight, and then I began a university degree to become a qualified teacher. The Montessori method was thoroughly inspiring and enjoyable and even helped me unblock my negative relationship with mathematics. The teacher-training programme, on the other hand, was immensely disappointing, with underlying themes mostly to do with time management, discipline, and targets. Regrettably, I don't recall any discussions on education's broader implications in the world.

My studies were interrupted by the birth of my first little boy. Within a few months, I heard rumours that Brockwood Park School was setting up 'The Children's Space' on two acres of enchanting grounds called Inwoods, just half a mile from its campus. I was twenty-six years old and with the immense responsibility of a new life in my hands. At this point, I couldn't help but ask myself what I had learnt from my childhood educational experiences that could shed light on an intelligent way forward into the world for this little lad. Here was an opportunity to negate the apparent hindrances to learning that I had experienced and enter a relationship with my son in which we were going to learn and grow together. Here was the chance to be part of a new project that questioned the harmful effects of conventional schooling and could put fundamental questions about life at the heart of its endeavours.

Commonly spotted in the bird boxes or the holly trees around the hammock, and memories of special friends

· 2 ·

The Children's Space

Loic and I, both former students, sat once again, this time as parents, in the 'Cloisters Sitting-Room' of Brockwood Park School with our son. With us were several Brockwood staff, most of whom were also parents of young children and included the director and the Spanish teacher, José, trained in primary education, as well as two sets of parents who were not part of Brockwood but who were later to become essential players in the pioneering era of this new education initiative.

I had Jonathan on my lap breastfeeding him in between naps while another baby, a little older, crawled within the circular area of seated attendees that had formed a wall of bodies and a safe space for her to play and move. This was one of the meetings in which the vision for 'The Children's Space' was discussed. I remember this small gathering's atmosphere more than the spoken words, visually marked by the two babies having their needs met with open acceptance and participation from everyone. The baby pushed around a little toy in front of us while the adults chatted, each one pausing for a moment when she had reached their legs to respond to her coos and babblings. There was an atmosphere of seriousness regarding the mission, as well as attention to this little being's equally important and wholly relevant presence in the room. I knew then that these were the people I wanted to work with, learn from, and have my child surrounded by.

Discussions continued without us and 'The Children's Space' opened in 1997 for a few days in the week for a handful of children. In the summer of 1998, when Jonathan was nearly two years old, we moved into a rented cottage just one and a half miles from Brockwood Park School. Loic looked after the maintenance and functioning of the facilities there part-time while I volunteered some hours on some days at The Children's Space at Inwoods, sometimes with Jonathan in tow and at other times while he was being looked after by a mature student of Brockwood Park. 'Mature students' were male or female volunteers from a number of European and other countries, usually in their twenties, perhaps taking a gap year after university or simply interested in Krishnamurti's educational approach, who assisted with the running of the various Brockwood departments in return for board and lodging.

There is a saying that goes, 'It takes a village to raise a child', an oft-quoted phrase which leads me to make a slight digression here, to say a few words about my thoughts on the nuclear family. In between my Travelling School experience and completing my Montessori training, I was an *au pair* for a family in Switzerland who had a young child and a baby. Not only was this a wonderful introduction to the magnificent Swiss mountain and lake landscapes, but it was also a valuable insight into the life of a well-functioning and financially stable family. The children had everything they needed: caring parents; toys; learning materials; a garden; a dog; good food. However, I would now tentatively suggest – and with no discredit to this lovely family – that perhaps that particular 'raising environment' lacked some broader richness for their elder child in not having other adults, i.e. other than her parents, to dilute the exclusively parental influences that are unavoidably absorbed by an admiring daughter. Parents can unwittingly (or not) seduce their children to their ways, values and interests. However, if it is possible to include other members of the family, other families, neighbours, carers and friends into the 'raising', then perhaps the variety of personalities and their assorted approaches to life would widen the child's outlook and provide a richer ground in which to question and learn. This shared raising could also offer a healthy variation and alternative to the sometimes intense and even taxing intimacy that can develop between parents and children.

So, with this nascent concern already somewhere in the back of my mind – and somewhat hesitantly at first – I handed over my initially reluctant child to a young woman from Brockwood whom admittedly I didn't know especially well, but in whom I sensed a gentleness and goodness that I could trust. She proved to be a most valuable contribution to Jonathan's upbringing for a short but vital period, as well as somebody I myself could learn from. Like many families in the West (unless one is surrounded by aunts and uncles, cousins and grandparents, and has firm roots within the locality), it is a challenge to avoid the 'nuclear family syndrome'. For this reason, I felt the added sense of urgency to somehow find or form a community setting.

Before moving to the area and into my volunteer role at The Children's Space, I was requested to present a topic to the five young children attending. I didn't know them well, so I decided to share the topic I was most interested in and most directly involved with at the time – Jonathan. I also believed a young baby in nappies could not be too far from the interest of this group of children, especially the alive, kicking, babbling cutie that he was, and I was hopeful that there would be enough questions to fuel the 'presentation'. Jonathan was a success, but so were the children in demonstrating their curiosity and care for the little fellow who sat amongst them on the classroom rug. It seemed our interests matched, and this 'matching of interests' became a key criterion for many of my sessions with children from then on.

From that experience my apprenticeship evolved with this little group into the world of teaching and learning. I had had some experience during my teacher training and travels of groups of children in classroom learning environments, but nothing as intimate as this. I watched José closely, admiring his capacity for playfulness and spontaneity with the children while ensuring that there was some direction and rhythm to the day. He also had a gentle firmness that seemed sometimes necessary for mediating a group of assertive youngsters, as the following account illustrates.

It was snack-time. The table was set, and there were only just enough chairs for the number of children in the room.

Daniella sat down on one chair and put her teddy on the adjacent one next to her, but, as a result, Carrie didn't have a chair to sit on. I'll just explain this to Daniella, I thought, she will understand. "No", was her emphatic response, followed by the assertion that the chair was definitely for *her* teddy and no one else. "Look", I said, "Where is Carrie going to sit?". There was no persuasive argument or emotional outpouring; she just looked me straight in the eye and said, very factually, that her soft friend needed this chair. I was almost convinced that she had a point. But just as her calm obstinacy began to fluster me, José stepped in, and without any concern that there would be a battle, acknowledged Daniella's desire while *at the same time* pulling up a box, putting her inanimate friend gently on it and pulling out the empty seat for Carrie to sit down on. "Now everyone has a seat", José said factually with his swift, caring, practical action to illustrate. It was clearly not a case for negotiating as far as José was concerned, and to my surprise, Daniella did not appear to be at all troubled by that.

One of the most challenging tasks for an educator and a parent is to intelligently navigate children's complex individual drives, deciphering what is a 'need' and what is a 'desire', without undermining either, and all in the context of the collective. Whether it be the classroom or the family unit, there will be multiple individual demands ranging from the absolute necessities in life to the most inconsequential ones, with all the range and richness of whims and fancies mixed in. Educators and parents have experimented with various approaches to tackle this challenge, ranging from total control of the child's development and interests at one end of the scale and complete autonomy, whatever the motive, at the other. Perhaps any point on this scale could be justifiable for a particular circumstance; it becomes a problem though when that point is a fixed one and has no relevance to the situation but just to a belief or pedagogical stance.

Discipline, autonomy, assertiveness, conformity, non-conformity etc. may all have their place in life, but our questions of knowing when and how to deploy these as strategies can be confusing as we try to match our observations of a real and present situation with our stances and expectations. Is it possible to observe and respond to a child's needs with respect to the group and circumstance without grasping for a devised method of sorts? Can we find the right way forward within the context of any given situation and in direct relationship with those involved? This is the educator's fundamental work, and why having only small groups of children in stress-free settings is more likely to make such work possible.

•

The Children's Space was in a small, converted barn on two acres of land surrounded by trees. There was also a dusty, derelict brick 'wash house' in one corner, a larger high-ceilinged barn used for wood storage in another corner and a magnificent mature oak tree under which many playful happenings would later take place. The 'Small Barn' consisted of a handful of children, plus two adults: José and Susan. Here there was the potential to develop a unique relationship with each child in which personalities and idiosyncrasies could be seen, interests listened to, emotions respected and impulsive actions gently attended to, all in the context of a caring and safe place for learning, not limited to the accumulation of knowledge.

Joseph, for example, had been attending The Children's Space with his mother. He didn't want to be there without her, and all agreed that it was important to respect the natural progression of separation and not try to sever the 'cord' prematurely. However, it had already been nearly six months. Joseph appeared happy and engaged both inside and outside of the space, whether mum was at his side or not, but any attempt for her to leave the site brought screams of disapproval. One day, after witnessing again the secure friendships and excellent connection with José, mum bit the bullet and decided to let José hold him so that she could head home without him chasing after her. She left quickly (though having warned him this was going to happen); Joseph cried, José acknowledged his pain with tenderness, and after several minutes of emotional release, Joseph went happily off to play. Was this a violation – a dominant adult complicit with others, providing him with no choice in the matter?

In this case, maybe not. That evening Joseph told his mum that he had been crying all those times before because he wanted her to stay, though he knew that he didn't really need her there; he said the crying worked, so he just continued. I do not think Joseph was manipulative. I suspect there was genuine discomfort from a form of separation anxiety, but he had managed to avoid that discomfort each time by crying out and stopping the separation from happening. I would suggest that in this particular instance of *holding* a difficult sensation, José and his mum supported him to go through that discomfort and come out the other side in one peaceful piece, thus breaking an unnecessary cycle of dependence that had developed for whatever reason.

•

After a while, my role in The Children's Space became somewhat more 'official', and with that grew an increase in the demands and questions of parents on me. Most of the time I did not have clear answers and I was embarrassed by my flustered responses and overall 'pretence' of knowing. Education is a multifaceted field, and each child is a unique and complex being with their own conditioned or instinctive 'tool-bag' of different ways of meeting life. For most parents, it was their first child attending an educational space. They wondered or were sometimes positively anxious about when their child should start reading, whether they were articulate enough for their age, creative enough, physically active enough, too quiet or too noisy, too boisterous or too timid. They wanted to know how I was going to teach x, y and z. Seemingly they wanted reassurance, direction and proven methods as guarantees.

One day, one such parent asked me a question that I could not confidently answer, but this time, after some thoughtful consideration, I admitted to her quite frankly that I didn't know. I remember the surprised "Oh!" followed by a soft smile, and then the discussion we both entered into about her child, her observations, my observations, and the inevitable unknowing that both of us were facing. I stepped off my pedestal with her helping hand onto the same ground, and, from then on, we both walked side by side, exploring together questions related to teaching and learning.

Authority in its various forms has a wicked way of creating façades and barriers between human beings. Either we elevate ourselves to 'all-knowing' or we follow others whom we ourselves have put there. Our exchanges then risk taking on a hierarchical relationship in which questioning is seen as an insult rather than a learning opportunity. This is not to say that expertise and understanding in a field aren't necessary; without specialised knowledge, we would not have the technical advances in the world that we see today. However, 'experts' are mostly the result of specialisation in an area and therefore limited if one considers the overall complexity and interconnectedness of life. Is it possible to come off our specialist pedestals and then meet each other in that field of not-knowing?

I began to see that education needed to be a holistic endeavour where, with good reason and within reason, specialisation and knowledge have their place. And where they may be integrated within the context of *who* a child is, including their individual circumstances, the limitations of the school's setting, the locality, and the wider world. With this in mind, I aimed to walk side by side with children, parents, teachers, colleagues, trustees, bursar, facility manager, cook, gardener, cleaner and anyone else who would join what I felt had the makings of a unique 'education village'.

When I found a rare fungus on a walk in the woods,
named it and made a dance based on how it was
shaped with a friend

· 3 ·

Walking Together

It was a beautiful September day, 1999, and the beginning of a new 'school' year. It was also the beginning of a new phase in the history of Inwoods. The 'Children's Space' was expanding, and with it my role and responsibilities. Throughout the summer, parents helped to renovate the first half of the 'Big Barn'. Today, the six oldest children who had grown out of the Small Barn marked the occasion with a celebratory march; holding candles and flowers, they walked in a line from their old classroom to their newly decorated and furnished one on the other side of the grounds. We inaugurated the space with a fun cooperative team-challenge of building a standing character out of newspaper with only tape to hold it together.

This day was also a turning point in my contributions to this growing education village. I was both nervous and excited. Having had the role of an assistant I was now assigned a group of my own. There were hardly any teaching resources to draw on for ideas. The space was equipped with the bare minimum of materials: some books, stationery, basic art supplies, cloths and cushions, a couple of tables with chairs and a sink. I felt as if I had a blank canvas in front of me with just the essentials and these fresh young minds with whom to collaborate on something together. The responsibility felt immense. I did not have much of a plan though I was clear that I didn't want to coerce the children into taking up any of my offerings or manipulate their behaviour in any way. I didn't want any of them to develop fixed notions with regards to their capacity for learning.

A collaborative spirit seemed to be in the fabric of the whole place. Whether it was with hammers and nails to get the Big Barn renovated, with paints and brushes to make it attractive, or with words of encouragement and reflection from the parents as they entrusted me with their children; everyone had a part to play in creating a unique environment for learning to happen. Sallie, Amanda, and Colleen were inspiring teachers, bringing their artistic contributions and songs to all the children. José had moved back to Spain at this point, having brought the school to this important phase.

And so, this was how we worked together, building relationships day by day, with each one finding a meaningful way to contribute. But it wasn't always easy. My subject strengths were with the arts and crafts and less with the abstract knowledge areas, and I had a quiet, shy voice when it came to parent and 'working group' meetings. As there was no classroom clock, that first week I set about preparing blank clock-faces, acquired some real clock mechanisms, and invited the children to make their personalised clock and one for the new space, thus combining art, design and mathematics into something useful and hands-on. This offering went down very well, but it had been a lot of work to prepare, and the children's abilities ranged from those who could write their numbers to those who couldn't, and those who took to the task with persistent independence to those who cheerfully engaged only when my hands were there to help – and having first coaxed them away from doing cartwheels across the room.

I soon discovered the challenge of supporting this mixed age and ability group of children with reading, writing and mathematical learning. An art-related activity often won most of the children's interest, with the whole group joining in with enthusiasm. Splashing paint around and exploring colour never seemed to bore them, and I think there was something in the social opportunities it created that was also appealing. However, for most of them, practising writing or doing numeracy exercises did not sustain the same level of group engagement. A different approach was needed.

Eren was nearly nine years old, and despite my efforts to bring literacy activities into his learning world, he still didn't know how to read or write. I was a little worried – though his parents weren't worried at all! They saw an alive, witty and happy child, and they felt the penny would drop in his own time. It did. I was sitting with a couple of children with a small A4 whiteboard practising matching sounds with their correct letter representations. One child gave me some letters to display on the board and asked me to read the 'word' that these letters created. It was a pseudoword and a rather silly sounding one that made us all giggle. On hearing the fun, a few other children gravitated towards us, including Eren, who also started to demand the 'words' made by ever-lengthening strings of letters that included x's, y's and z's. Eren was hooked. This child, who thrived on humour and fun, laughed and loved the power these letter pictures could have. He, too, wanted to unlock the sound/letter code, and in a few months, Eren was reading fluently. After he left Inwoods at age eleven, apparently his reading test result at secondary school was calculated to be that of an average fifteen-year-old.

Eren's parents were a gift to my evolving understanding of a child. They didn't worry about him, and they didn't expect him to meet national curriculum targets. Out of careful observation and deep respect, they trusted in their child's innate (and sometimes quirky) capacity to learn and to enjoy learning. I think they trusted *me* because I was not claiming to know or understand Eren more than they did, and also because we had entered into an open and friendly relationship in which we walked this education journey with their son together.

Speaking of trust, where was *my* child in all of this? Jonathan was in another part of the two-acre 'learning-village', in the Small Barn with Sallie and Amanda and a few other younger children who had joined the community. He was used to my presence at home and while assisting on the grounds, so it was a new experience for him to have me on site but not at the immediate call of his needs and wishes. I remember him initially wandering over to the Big Barn and pressing his nose to the window, looking in to see what I was doing. Sometimes I could nip out and steal a hug then direct him somewhat reluctantly back to his group; at other times I would only manage a wave through the windowpane or blow him a kiss, and it was often an *older* child who would take his hand and walk him back down the playground path. Admittedly it was painful for us both – him being just short of three years old – but I also felt the circumstances supported these little moments of independence. Jonathan, despite his age, seemed to acknowledge my predicament and his teachers gave him the freedom to observe it, to say 'hi', to find out what mummy was up to, to see that she was okay and rather too occupied to get much out of her at that moment – and then to be affectionately escorted back to his playmates by the trusted hand of another child.

•

There was still no internet use from the school to parents at the time and so no email correspondence. Important and urgent information was relayed through the community of adults via a 'phone-tree'. The messenger phoned the first person at the top of the list, who then had to pass the message to the next one down and so on. Invariably the news didn't reach the end in a timely manner, if at all, and if it did, one couldn't rely on it being an intact piece of information. Sometimes we attempted starting the message at both ends of the list, but this brought extra confusion to the missive, with people receiving the message twice, the second being a variant of the first – it's a wonder we managed to coordinate anything at all!

Without the internet at the beginning, and in spite of it later on, school gatherings, in whatever format, became essential forums for sharing ideas, eliciting help, and delegating. More importantly, they helped build relationships so that one didn't get caught up in the pettiness of, for example, blaming someone, and could instead focus on what was vital and urgent. Parents, teachers, children and younger siblings would regularly picnic together on the school grounds like a big family and enjoy work parties for tidying the place and creating play features. These gatherings came about somewhat spontaneously, but as the school grew in size, more careful coordination was needed to ensure everyone felt included in some way and for it to become a shared event.

When it comes to communication, if we dare to look a little closer, we will see that we all have a part to play in misunderstandings and misinformation, whether it be a trivial matter or something of greater significance. I was learning to apologise readily, strive for improved communication strategies where it made sense, and beginning to recognise – in the mirror of my relationships – when I might be wasting energy on my self-centred concerns. It helped to have this pioneering group of families, many of whom had come to Inwoods via word-of-mouth and knew each other already, so non-conflictual exchanges came naturally and easily. A foundation of friendships was formed among the parents, which Loic and I embraced and appreciated for the equal footing that we all found ourselves on in this challenge to educate our children and live a sane life. I'm told by several of them now how their friendships deepened in the context of the school's intentions and happenings.

But it wasn't always rosy. I remember one frequent cause for contention was food. One parent was adamant that there should be no sugar on the grounds at Inwoods. As the school was not providing meals then (that would come a few years later), children came with packed lunches. They sat indoors or outside in friendship clusters, curious about each other's lunch box contents and spontaneously sharing and exchanging items. Everyone agreed that wholesome meals were a fundamental necessity for healthy growth, but several grey areas in terms of ingredients didn't get everyone's consensus for 'banning'. This particular parent considered 'healthy' snack bars containing processed sugar alternatives (such as date juice) or a home-made cake with considerably reduced raw cane sugar content, to be a cause of concern for her daughter's wellbeing – a daughter who was now seeing and sometimes receiving these 'indulgent' items from her friends. This mother was right to raise the alarm, and I would not have been the only one agreeing that sugar is an incredibly addictive and unhealthy substance if used carelessly or to excess. However, while some parents were inspired to pay more attention to the food they were giving their children, others felt she was obsessive and dictatorial in the manner she was insisting her views be adhered to by the community.

My rose-tinted glasses were knocked right off my nose as I saw irritation and unnecessary statements being circulated and leaking into the atmosphere of the place. It was my first experience of divisive thinking within the context of the school's endeavours, resulting in tension among some people. I imagined some parents felt their adequately good habits were being threatened and didn't want any 'policing' of their child's lunchbox. I was aware of my own unfortunate bias for sweet products while also in agreement with the health concerns raised. But two things were clear: I didn't want to fall out with anyone over this school issue, nor did I want to impose my personal view on the children. So, what was my role when sitting amongst the children during lunchtime, with this new knowledge of their parents' mixed expectations?

It is possible a 'democratic school model' would have put the issue to a school vote to include all members (and particularly the children). Each food item may have been voted in or out, and in this case, I imagine there would have been more hands in favour of keeping certain sugary items in lunchboxes. I was not familiar with democratic approaches in schools at the time, which I have now grown to support and better understand; however, I do have some questions and reservations with the tendency for group peer pressure and majority-decision games. Does action arising out of such majority votes equate to 'right' action?

In fact, the children I sat with for lunch had the healthiest lunchboxes that I had ever seen, as well as a healthy level of ease with speaking, sharing, and chatting together. I don't recall the details of our conversations, though I did raise the topic of sugar with them, which included looking at the various disguises sugar took in snack bars, biscuits, and home-made cakes, for example, and chatting about the yumminess of sugar and what our bodies need and don't need. The best I felt I could do was to open up the dialogue regarding food and raise awareness of some of its issues, but without claiming orthodoxy for any assumed 'facts'. We also chatted about differing opinions and how we may influence each other with our likes and dislikes.

Such conversations with children don't have the orderly manner and sometimes feigned politeness that one gets with adults. It can be quite a chaotic process with children interrupting each other with exclamatory gestures and words, and attempts at wittiness often ending in downright silliness. I often wondered whether anything fruitful was arising out of my 'awareness raising' attempts amid all that. But, over time, I learned to relax and sensitively enter the children's social world when appropriate, and then to ask some important questions without being too missionary about it. Some interesting reflections made by the children themselves were brought out in this way, allowing me to learn in return. I also enjoyed witnessing other teachers with more playful temperaments than mine, connecting with the children on relevant issues in more spontaneous ways.

Fortunately, tensions among the parent community regarding packed lunches seemed to dissipate, and I didn't experience any personal antagonisms. Still, it made me aware of how fragile relationships can be, and our tendency as humans to quickly seek mutually supportive allegiances rather than sustain an all-inclusive element of doubt and questioning. As the years went by, I was learning to navigate and facilitate the community's varying opinions – of which there were many! This seemed to me to be a crucial aspect of this education project. It was also a very challenging one.

Divisive thinking, rampant in our society, is a significant cause of all forms of conflict across the globe; a new way of relating and working together is urgently needed, overriding our differences of opinions and cultures. I see no point in a child accumulating so much knowledge and skills if, at the end of their education journey, they use it to undermine others or rally support for their self-centred activities. As educators and parents, we also have a responsibility to see that the environment in which the children grow up is a representation of an intelligent way of relating to one another – not in opposition to others, not making problems, not arguing about who is right and who isn't right. But also, not trying to create a utopia!

Our accumulated knowledge is important but also *limited*, especially if we have little understanding or awareness of the psychological aspects of our being. To educate beyond the limitations of mere information and technical skills requires providing the children and ourselves with the space and opportunities to learn about ourselves: how we think; why we think in a particular way; how we feel; why we feel; what motivates us; our fears; our jealousies and other emotions. I don't propose this as any kind of psychological analysis but more as an invitation to observe these inner movements in action while we are interacting with others.

Thus far there was hardly anything utopian about Inwoods: the children kept us on our toes with their vibrant energy, their emotions, and various complex needs. Entering the children's world – observing it, feeling it, respecting it, loving them for it – was key to the more holistic approach to learning that we wanted to have. Two worlds needed to meet, that of the adult and that of the child, and without any opposition whatsoever.

*Blackberry picking and finding other edible things from around the
school, like gooseberries, raspberries and blackcurrants*

· 4 ·

Meeting of Two Worlds

Our adult worlds are often busy places with many responsibilities that require planning and organising, and as a result our minds are filled with endless thought. We strive for order and forward-thinking while also spending time cleaning up our affairs and reminiscing on past troubles. In coping with a life of suppressed or strong emotion and anxiety, we look for some decompression in the form of a distraction of sorts. Young children's worlds, on the other hand, do not carry the burden of responsibility and striving; they don't plan their actions, they just act, react and follow their impulses, their *in-the-moment* unselfconscious needs and fancies. Order is less of a thing to cling to, resulting in a trail of half-finished and dipped-into mini-projects and creative happenings.

These worlds may sound wide apart, but in fact, they have a lot more in common. Adults and children respond well to rhythm and routines regarding sleep, meals and rest or movement. Everyone has cravings and aversions of varying intensities. Most of us, young or old, need to be touched, held and appreciated. We all experience emotions such as fear, anger, sadness and joy. We all suffer. We all want to be loved.

I've heard it said that the varying temperaments and learning-styles of children tend to become more unified when they are in their teens, making it somewhat easier to teach a group of sixteen-year-olds than a group of six-year-olds. I'm not sure if this is the natural progression of the child's state or if it is due to the factory-type of mass education that trains children to conform and perform in a particular way. However, I do remember Stefan – a part-time teacher, who taught a small group of children at Inwoods on some days and a small group of teenagers at Brockwood on other days – say that it was a relative 'doddle' to teach the *teenagers*. He would introduce a writing theme, they would discuss it politely together, and then they all got their heads down to independently writing their pieces while he would sit back and enjoy the quiet, focused atmosphere.

With the Inwoods children, however, it was another atmosphere altogether. First, a chunk of time would be taken up facilitating a squabble over the seating arrangement. Then, just as the teacher was to get started on his introduction, there would be a needed drink of water, or a trip to the loo, or a hunt for a sharper pencil. Once personal necessities had been sorted, and the intro presented, the children would mix on-topic exchanges with random banter before some heads were finally down on task – though loo trips, water top-ups, and stationary issues, among others, continued to send heads rising and turning. Throughout the session, the teacher had to facilitate the children's physical needs, emotional moods, distractions, and varying academic levels and engagement with the task. There was no time to put one's feet up because every child's response was an important one – whether related to the lesson or an unmet need or sensation.

It's important to note that Stefan's sessions were quite structured, and one could argue that all the commotion and responses of the children were a reaction to this imposition on them. Possibly to some extent, though the children mostly communicated that they liked his classes. Different teachers over the years had varying styles of teaching or guiding groups of children in their learning. Whatever approach was used, there would still be impulses and expressions of need of varying intensities in all setups.

Whatever the circumstances – and whether it be a need or something else – children move, talk, argue, laugh, cry and assert themselves in all manner of ways frequently perplexing the adults around them. As an educator, what is our relationship with all that? How do we support the learning of essential skills and the acquisition of the necessary knowledge to get along in this world, while at the same time respecting the emotional, social and physical life of the maturing child?

Social and classroom spaces can be dominated by personality traits and the idiosyncrasies of the children it contains. Inwoods seemed to attract many vibrant, interesting and 'complex' characters. Or was it that it just didn't quash them through school-wide '*behaviour management strategies'* and dictatorial adults? There were no reward stickers, behaviour charts or punishments to manipulate the children into responding to our plans, or deliberate ways to 'correct' their sentiments to match our own. This meant that educators needed to observe what was going on for a particular child more closely, especially when there was friction or resistance. It meant connecting more deeply with their inner turmoil and desires rather than brushing them aside as something inconvenient and contrary to one's views. It meant the hard and humble work of recognising one's prejudices and ideas about how a child *should* be or *should* become or *should* behave. 'Should' was altogether a word that was sparingly used and challenged within the culture of the school.

A small setting with small classes, and a small team looking after the place, naturally gave rise to less rigidity and more of the spontaneity that one might find in a family environment, though habits can still get in the way. I remember watching one new teacher to the team, who had come from a 'mainstream' teacher-training programme (in which crowd control would have been expected) summon a group of ten children to line up in front of the gate before heading out. Queuing can have the undesirable effect of creating rivalry between young children as they compete for status by being at the front. I asked her why they had to line up, given how few and safely close together they were with her. She admitted that she couldn't see the point other than to satisfy some notion of order and feeling of control. Queues for large numbers can help provide a visual cue to a physical solution of getting everyone through a gate one by one rather than a scramble. But in this case, all the children were in earshot for a calm reminder to take care of each other when passing through the narrow space. In this situation, one would not be controlling the children, but rather inviting them to organise themselves – and for the important reason that it would also kindly benefit others.

On another occasion, after a couple of weeks of employment at Inwoods, Lynne felt ready to independently facilitate the learning of a small group of mixed-aged children between six and eight years old. She had carefully planned an activity and went to gather her group with expectation and promise. However, most of them weren't on the same enthusiastic wavelength as her, and some were freely vocal about it: "Boring", "No", "Don't want to", they said. They came across as downright rude, and Lynne left the chaotic space distraught and tearful.

At the time, the most reassuring thing I could point out was that she didn't know the children that well and they didn't know her; a close relationship had not yet formed between them. These children had not been trained into obedience (fortunately), and they had not yet learnt the art of expression without hurting (though who has!). The dialogues that followed brought some lightness and understanding of the incident. In her reflective state, Lynne spoke of the constant praise she had received in her life for being a 'good' and 'capable' student and the expectations she now had to 'perform'. "People have told me I will be an excellent teacher", she said, with the tone of a somewhat bruised identity. "But are we always excellent?" I replied. "Foolish at times too, I think. I know I can be both."

The children also had the opportunity to share *their* reactions, without being reprimanded, and to hear how their teacher had felt and responded. They all laughed about it, and in doing so, grew that little bit more connected with each other via an authentic raising of those inner movements that we are all susceptible to. Those chats brought two worlds together and offered an insight into so much more than what the original intention for learning had been. Lynne also learned about what the children were interested in, what they were capable of, and how to marry her ideas and plans with their temperaments, imaginations, questions and plans. The children began to trust in Lynne's endeavour to see who they were, not how she expected them to be.

·

Children's imaginations are more than just the fantasising of fairy tale worlds or the capacity to think out of the box. For the very young, I discovered that the boundaries of reality and non-reality could be somewhat blurred. One morning, during a break-time when some of the children had wandered into the Big Barn, I happened to enter the cloakroom area just at the start of some brewing commotion within the classroom. Curious to know what was going on, I paused for a moment and peered through the interior windows and the slightly ajar door. I observed some of the older children teasing five-year-old Jake. Nothing majorly unpleasant appeared to be taking place, as far as my adult perspective could tell. There was a lot of giggling and minimal contact, with one particular child seeming to lead the 'play'. But, Jake was not laughing. It seemed he was the target of their bit of fun. After a moment, I stepped in to support his exclamations of disapproval, and the children moved off outside in frenetic energy, unawares.

Later that evening, to my horror, Jake had told his mother that he had been punched in the stomach by one of the children, though he couldn't say who it was. The next day I spoke with all of them individually, encouraging an honest account of their interactions with Jake and what they observed of the others. Nobody owned up to the punch, and from how they shared with me, I felt they were honest. So was Jake lying? I spoke about this to a friend (who also happened to be the parent of the child most vocal in the teasing) and she suggested that Jake may have experienced the children's mockery as vividly as a punch in the stomach. He wasn't lying; to him, the unpleasant feeling was a punch – that was his reality.

This episode gave me another window into a child's life and the limitations of one's perspectives. Whether Jake was lying or not, or my friend was right or not, it made me more careful about interpreting children's behaviour. In the search for facts, I discovered their actions are not so black and white, and that children move and behave in unpredictable ways by forces that we don't fully understand. In many cases, it is probably a hindrance to jump too quickly to conclusions about what we perceive. It may even be a danger to look elsewhere to have one's opinions confirmed. I'm sure there is a lot to glean from the many books and experts talking or writing about the development of a child. However, I chose then to keep observing, to keep an open mind as much as possible, and respectfully let these individuals' lives unfold with less interference from my projections and other people's ideas.

•

Inwoods was attempting to create an environment free of fear. That is to say, the fear that comes from deliberate strategies to control behaviour that might also undermine the children's endeavours or mishaps. As a result, many of the children were rather bold in their actions. I remember being convinced by five-year-old Aura that it was her sixth birthday that day, which resulted in me getting the whole school to sing happy birthday. She had brought all her little friends in on the prank – which wasn't really a prank. While they made pretend mud cakes and presents, I ran about coordinating a formal recognition of this 'special' day, as we did with all birthdays. Aura and all the children gaily lapped up my gullibility until the very (and rather embarrassing) end.

Lizzie was also rather gutsy. She started coming to Inwoods at the age of four, initially just a few days a week like many of the children, then consistently four days a week until she was eleven and ready to move on to secondary education. Her fifth day in the week was a 'home-ed' (education at home) day. Lizzie's parents were fully committed to the school's endeavours to develop trusting and open relationships between parents, children and the Inwoods team. Lizzie herself had a particularly close relationship with her teacher Shayla, who worked with her for several years. During one session,

Shayla was pointing out to a group of children that disrupting someone's flow by interrupting with one's own ideas wasn't helping the learning atmosphere. Lizzie responded by saying, "Shayla, you do that too". Shayla recounted that Lizzie didn't come across as deliberately rude or disrespectful; she was just stating what she saw as a fact. According to Shayla, Lizzie's frankness and affectionate relationship with her prompted her to also reflect on how she was regularly interacting with the children.

Another example of 'fearlessness' of a more hazardous nature, is Rishi's introduction to a new playground game of dare. He would dare one child to trip up another one, not too seriously, but enough to be annoying and intimidating with the risk of hurting nonetheless. Most of the children refused, but on one occasion a victim of this dare came to me, fortunately not hurt but clearly put out by Rishi's influence over his younger friend, who despite their friendship had been persuaded to push him. Just telling Rishi that his behaviour was not acceptable wasn't having much of an impact. He said it was a game, a kind of joke, and so felt it was ok to do. Punishing him would likely have made him more resentful and prone to continuing such games in secret, whereas he was quite open and public about his interactions, as were, fortunately, many of the children.

Rishi and I had already had other conversations about some intimidating behaviour and had come to appreciate the reflective process using writing – a medium of expression he was confident with. I suggested he spend a few minutes alone and write down what he feels about the situation that arose and caused this child to be upset. He rather quickly scribbled a note saying, *"I shouldn't do this game because the children are too young to get that it is just a joke, and I don't mean for them to hurt others."* When I read this, I wondered if Rishi was still passing the 'fault' onto the younger children rather than seeing the root of his own actions and their implications. I asked him if he was implying that it would be ok to make this 'joke' with older children because they wouldn't actually hurt another child, but then what was the point of this 'game/joke'? What was he really gaining from it? Both of us thought for a moment, and he said that it was the element of risk that he liked – the risk that his request would actually be carried out. He agreed that he was receiving some pleasure out of this risk which is why he called it a game, which led to a discussion regarding games and jokes, and whether it was better to make these enjoyable for all rather than for oneself at the expense of others. He went away on his own volition to add this risk element of his 'game' to his written reflections.

I sensed Rishi appreciated this explorative process of thinking something through together, rather than being pressured to think in a particular way. I was sincerely wondering what his internal drives were and how much he was conscious of them, so I learned something too. Thankfully, he didn't play this game again.

It goes without saying, as with all primary schools – where children are learning to navigate their individual emotions in the context of a shared space – in the history of twenty Inwoods years there were some unpleasant interactions between children, friendship break-ups, particular children not getting along with others, and exclusive behaviour, which the staff attempted to address as constructively and respectfully as possible in all manner of ways. On many occasions, solutions were found, and friendships were restored and deepened – with or without our support – but there were also occasions in which a restoration of sorts wasn't quickly arrived at. A few parents criticised us for not having stricter measures in place, though children rarely asked for these for themselves. Needless to say, the outcome of relational conflicts hinged somewhat on the attitudes of the children involved, tainted by their parent's perspective, and dependent on the quality of communication between everyone. When one mother wrote to me and shared her concern that her daughter didn't seem to be 'gelling' with one of the girls in her group, she also added:

> *"Susie is a funny one – when I tell her that I perhaps could help her with her problems, in whatever way she wants me to, she says that she actually likes to have some problems and that she finds it exciting to go to school to see what happens about them that day."*

Friendships are an immensely significant aspect of a child's education. Indeed, when children are asked about school, friends are often mentioned as their main reason for attending, and when that is not going well and neglected it often becomes the reason for not wanting to attend. Much of the time children are preoccupied by thoughts and concerns with respect to the daily challenge of relating. At Inwoods, we gave deliberate time and space for relationships to develop and deepen, aware that with experiences of closeness and honest interactions with others at this tender young age, this is what would be valued and nurtured as they journeyed through life. One example of this is illustrated below by Vicky who is reflecting on her experience of 'friendship' while attending her first year of secondary school:

"Inwoods was not like a school. At least, I did not think of it as a school. I found the most amazing people there and built unique relationships with people I never want to forget. Those, I realise, were an incredible privilege that hardly any state school children have experienced. Now I am at a state Secondary school, I can see how different friends and relationships are. It is, in fact, almost a crime by punishment to have any friendship with a boy; he must be an enemy or your boyfriend. When I first started Secondary, this was crazy to me as a few of my best friends were boys. I was constantly told I had a boyfriend because I talked to one of my best friends. I thought this was sad that people could not speak to someone of the opposite sex without being made fun of. However, at Inwoods, this was never a problem; everyone was friends no matter their gender.

I've also noticed how intense many friendships are at Secondary school, so intense and untrustworthy. Having a 'best friend' is probably one of the most dangerous things you can have in a state school: the rumours, people feeling left out, constantly in fear of losing said 'best friend'. To keep this kind of 'best friend' (a term used very loosely), you have to talk to them and text each other all the time. If you don't keep in contact every minute of every day, they could find a new 'best friend'. All my genuine best friends from Inwoods live over an hour away. Even if I haven't had the chance to talk to them, I never feel the need to drop them. And never have I considered they would get a new close friend either because

*the trust we have built in that relationship is so strong. I
would trust them completely. Never have they lied, or have I
felt they were keeping something. These kinds of relationships
I built at Inwoods are something I will remember my whole
life. And I will remember those people forever."*

•

Children can be deeply reflective and questioning about life.
If we enter a bit into their world of ponderings, we see how
connected they can also be with ours. Leah was seven years
old, and the two of us were sitting together with a few other
children at the lunch table. The topic of 'love' came up in
their chit-chat of giggles. I asked if there was any difference
between the feeling of being 'in love' and just 'love'. I was
moved by young Leah's insightful response; she said the
'in love' feeling was something that you kept wanting and
looking for; however, 'love' was just there all the time.
Some months later, I discovered that her parents were going
through a break-up in their marriage which eventually
resulted in her father moving in with another partner.

Yoël, my younger son, also around the age of seven,
joined me one afternoon while relaxing propped up on my
bed, leisurely looking out through the window at the sky and
treetops. It was one of those few moments of inactivity and
quietness. He came and laid next to me, and we were both
quiet like this for some time. Then all of a sudden, he stated,
"There is no such thing as time". I tentatively asked him
what he meant, and he responded that there are calendars
and watches and stuff that humans have made to create

time, but actually, time doesn't exist. I didn't risk adding anything of my own view as I felt there was a freshness of something that he was perceiving at that moment that I didn't want to interfere with. Perhaps he was experiencing the timeless beauty of life that one can be in touch with, if not caught in the measurement and suffering of time passing. Or maybe it was something else. Mostly though, we fill each moment of a child's day with activities, agenda-packed conversations and time-specific goals in which quiet intervals of perception are lost.

*Turning over logs and finding a moist collection of slugs,
snails and woodlice, known as "Woody Kingdoms"*

· 5 ·

Working With 'What Is'

Beneath the adult's façade of politeness and aside from his or her pent-up outbursts of frustration and hurt, there are responses to life ranging from downright foolishness to outright brilliance. As with children, adults also have feelings, emotions, perceptions, insights and personalities that need respecting, as well as learning that needs supporting. Whether a parent or a staff member, Inwoods was rich with adult characters from all walks of life, all of us working within the constraints of the school's infrastructure and the inevitable imperfections of our being.

How much does the *appearance* of greatness sway us? The Internet offers a window into some of the world's most amazing innovations as well as the lives and achievements of incredibly talented people. Within the field of education, some well-crafted school websites are promising the best educational environments with teachers who possess 'outstanding' abilities and qualifications. How true to reality those websites are is one question, but in any case, what if one's education initiative *doesn't* have the same resources, the financial backing, 'expertise' or necessary infrastructure to make the place 'brilliant' in all respects? And who is to decide on the criteria for measuring that brilliance? Measurement in itself is often a source of ongoing tension and conflict in an educational organisation.

What if, instead of aspiring to greatness which is somewhere 'out there', we work together with 'what is' and evolve together from a place of direct observation, without comparison, and within the context of our immediate surroundings and possibilities? Evolving *not* to achieve some idea of a brilliant end, but to allow brilliance and beauty, in all its guises, to unfold and be visible within the here-and-now of one's circumstances.

Inwoods' initial intention was to have a place for the children of Brockwood Park's school staff – not least because those staff with children were already wanting to 'do' education differently. A few other families from the local area with similar interests were invited to join, bringing a more vibrant social group to the space. Once one room became too small for the number of children, another space was converted, and then expanded with educational resources and play features gradually increasing as numbers rose and funds allowed for this. There were many fundraising initiatives and work-parties to develop the grounds and improve the provision, which included creating a striking ecological strawbale classroom. Teachers had to work beyond their contractual hours to create and recreate the teaching and learning spaces, coming in during some weekends and holidays to add their hands and hearts to these endeavours.

We relied on donated materials and recycled items, as well as on the enthusiasm of volunteers and parents lending a helping hand, which sometimes resulted in brilliant and much appreciated initiatives.

Between 1999 and 2003, Inwoods went through two headteachers, various other teachers and volunteers arrived or departed, and the rest of the Big Barn was converted to provide one large open-plan classroom with a kitchen, toilets and cloakroom entrance. I gave birth to another baby boy who was initially strapped to my back and then sometimes toddling about in tow as I assisted, contributed, observed and deepened my understanding of relationships in this complex and fragile unconventional education setting.

Then, in 2004, I was appointed headteacher following an in-depth assessment of the place by the director of one of Brockwood's sister schools in the US, also founded by J.Krishnamurti. Admittedly it was not a position I embraced with confidence and with open arms, but it was encouraged and supported by many people, perhaps in part because if I hadn't accepted, Inwoods would probably have closed.

When I accepted this headteacher role, I had no background in management, minimal experience with administrative tasks, and already had one of the greatest responsibilities in my hands – that of being a mother. But, for the school to continue, I had to take this on and find a way. The American school director during her visit supplied me with a number of their policies, their mission statements, their handbook and so on, as examples and templates to build on. I remember admiring her uncomplicated relationship with admin tasks, her upbeat energy and proactivity, and her encouraging smile. Finally, under the umbrella of The Krishnamurti Foundation Trust (KFT)[2], Ginny (my colleague) and I embraced the task that lay ahead of us – I with my title and passion, and she with her wisdom, experience, humour and outstanding endurance for hard work.

To our surprise, within a few weeks of my being appointed to the title, the Trust's governing body decided that they were going to close Inwoods at the end of the year and wrote a formal letter to all parents and staff to announce this. We were all confused; was it because those first children of Brockwood staff had grown out of the place, and so it no longer served its original purpose? Did they suddenly lack confidence in our ability for the task? Was it a financial concern? Parents wrote numerous letters supporting the school's endeavours and expressing their wish for a change of heart from the Trust. Ginny and I sat down together to try and make sense of it all. Given the parents' wishes and the ongoing dedication of the community, we submitted a proposal for a three-year feasibility period in which we would endeavour to make the school financially viable. It was approved.

Those three years were probably the hardest I ever worked in all my life. Ginny and I set in motion a drive and plan to be as financially frugal as possible and coordinate volunteers

---

2 The Krishnamurti Foundation Trust, of which Inwoods was part, was under the remote stewardship of a small group of Trustees with legal responsibility for the overall administration of the Brockwood campus and its activities. The onsite running of these activities was mandated by them to a group of directors, referred to as the 'Management Team'.

and parents to offer whatever skills and support they could. We taught, cooked, cleaned, fundraised, facilitated meetings, designed classroom spaces and prepared for our first major inspection. In 2006, miraculously, after a three-day in-depth visit (arriving a day earlier than expected), the government school inspection body, Ofsted, declared that we provided "High-quality education". Phew!

As a side note here, fortunately for us, Ofsted seemed to be less of a bureaucratic ordeal back in the day, and we were lucky to have a bunch of inspectors who appeared determined to make the scrutiny a relaxed and supportive affair. I distinctly remember discussing with one of them, her clipboard in hand, how we could legitimately tick the box that adults were using separate toilets to the children (a regulatory requirement for UK schools) because actually, we weren't; adults and children were sharing the one toilet for each space. "What about that house over there?" she asked me. 'That house' was on the premises and belonged to the Trust as accommodation for staff and mature students. Clearly it would be a troublesome inconvenience for a teacher to have to put on their wellies, abandon the children, and head out on an expedition across the playground each time they wanted to 'spend a penny'. But, *she* knew, that *I* knew, that she wasn't talking about us *actually* using those toilets… "*Could* you use them?" she asked me. "Well… yes…" "That will do", she interrupted, and quickly ticked that box.

Despite being about 20 years older than me, Ginny had the energy and dynamism of a youthful horse. She would get up in the early hours of the morning to scrub the potatoes so that they would be ready to go in the oven for baking while she was teaching later in the day. Then she would load the bread machine, set up the classroom and head back to Brockwood for the 'walking bus' back to Inwoods with the children. One would often see her going back and forth on the track between Inwoods and her lodgings at Brockwood, with a trolley filled with food and teaching supplies.

When she was present with the children, she would engage wholeheartedly with them, drawing out their stories (verbally and in writing) and participating enthusiastically with her own tales – of which there were many. She had a wonderful sense of humour and good spirit, even in the toughest of moments. In 2018 Leah's mother left a message at Inwoods, dropping by nearly ten years since her daughter's experience there (who is now at Cambridge). She said, "Inwoods really got Leah back into finding her love of learning with Ginny's guidance to 'unschool' her. Her time at Inwoods was formative."

'Unschooling' (or rather, 'deschooling') is a term that is now commonly used in the alternative education world. But how do you 'deschool' within a school? Many children came to Inwoods having tested out their local primary school to find that it *failed to respect who they were*. The level of fallout from their experience ranged from 'clamming up' when faced by an adult's questions to fear of any classroom setup or adult interactions, thus greatly hindering their learning potential. Sometimes it would take a few days or weeks for a child to feel safe to be themselves, and for others, it took much longer.

Darren's mum pulled him out of school as he was forced to sit on a designated small piece of carpet because he '*moved around too much*', which the school believed was a sign of some kind of disorder – he was only five! Nakos, aged six, was being threatened with the ultimate punishment: having to stay inside alone during playtime if he didn't work harder in class. Alice told her parents (in so many words) that she was fed up with all the stickers for best writer, best reader, tidiest person and so on, that were being awarded to her and others, causing tension among her classmates; she was only five years old but already recognised the manipulation at play and resulting unpleasant rivalry among her peers.

So much of the brilliant work of the Inwoods' teachers was in their patience and trust for those inner motivations to be restored. So much of their careful planning was in finding creative ways to maintain a respectful learning space for the diversity of learners it contained. Darren was given the freedom to move, but if stillness was sometimes necessary for the whole group (such as when a story was being read to everyone), he would listen attentively while his hands were at work drawing (his idea). Nakos requested *more* time outdoors in physical play and *blossomed* into more content-based learning when he was older. Alice, already an able reader when arriving at Inwoods, naturally dropped this previously coerced task for a while and took instead to the various art and craft activities offered, which she loved – sewing being a particular favourite. She picked up reading again on her own volition later, without any issues.

Gisela was a passionate educator. She came to Inwoods via Brockwood as a Mature Student, having spent some time in between studying Early Years Education in Spain. Her Hispanic background gave her a different angle on the academic learning targets of a child. In Spain, children aren't expected to be reading and writing at four, five, or six years old – not that Gisela felt they all couldn't, just that this wasn't the main emphasis of their learning. She placed *her* emphasis on what arose predominantly out of the children's own play. This was Gisela's brilliance.

The children played, and Gisela watched – then observed – came a little closer – watched some more – and if or when the moment was ripe, and a connection had been established, she asked a relevant question. In this way, creative ideas were developed, imaginations expanded, and resources brought out of inconspicuous places. Children were helped to share their thoughts and feelings with each other, to have a voice, to lead, to listen, and to participate. She uncovered their interests and wove them into offerings and invitations the following day, whether musical or mathematical, with paint or with letters, or to further build on all their imaginative creations and curious questions. Gisela saw herself as a person accompanying the children's development of themselves. Consequently, the children saw themselves developing because of themselves – not because of her.

Jeffrey joined the Inwoods teacher team after being a parent for a year. There are people who overflow with words, captivating the listener until the gist emerges, and those, of fewer words, who need to be sought out and asked a specific question because they actually but modestly have just as much to offer. Jeffrey was one of the latter, his answers taking their time to emerge and sometimes coming back as a question or reflection that seemed to deepen the exchange.

This had a remarkable effect on a number of the children's nervous systems (and adults'), calming them right down in his presence. Instead of being talked *at*, the children *tuned in*, and Jeffrey managed to create a timeless and fearless space for them to do this in, resulting in a reciprocated sense of respect and care.

Darshana, on the other hand, delighted in storytelling and in igniting all manner of artistic creations. She multitasked her way through an Inwoods' day with a persistent alert ear and eye on all activity corners of any given learning space, knowing when to step in and ask and guide, and when to step back and allow independent learning to unfold. Her level-headed temperament was well-suited to holding a group of children of mixed age and ability, all involved in differentiated tasks while also being mindful of social dynamics, individual responses, and the group's general interest level at any given time.

I could go on describing the talents and qualities of so many staff who passed through Inwoods: Shayla's passion for mathematics and her commitment to finding ways in which the children would engage without resistance; Stefan's detailed content-rich learning plans, delivered with humour and without stifling; Sam's rock-solid dedication and musical assemblies; Vince's delicious, nutritious meals; Amy's scriptwriting; Lynette's theatre productions; Frances' gentleness; Emily's organisation; Carla's creativity etc., etc. (to name just a few people and indeed not all of their qualities). Rather than following a formal training, staff were urged to tap into their latent or self-evident talents and skills, and to apply them unselfconsciously, within the context of a place that was inviting everyone to think together, to learn from each other, and to contribute to the development of the whole school, not just themselves.

However, working with 'what is' also requires working with each other's transient stumblings and fragilities, of which there are naturally many. At Inwoods, there were moods to contend with, irritations, upsets, and misunderstandings – all the stuff of life! There were also personal mini-crises such as breakdowns in relationships within the family home, a sick relative, a financial loss, a housing concern and suchlike, that could not always be 'left behind' at the school gate. As with the children, everyone had emotions and needed to be heard and respected. And everyone who joined us brought with them their own baggage and mindsets, their acquired tendency to think in certain ways, those complex aspects of day-to-day reality which could sometimes make communication discordant and messy.

The invitation contained in this educational endeavour was to see together 'what is' – the brilliance, the beauty, ugliness, the physical and mental blockages in oneself and others – without any judgement or comparison, without saying this is 'good' and that is 'bad'. The challenge was to see ourselves as we are, rather than some idea of how one 'should' be, and so to create an environment of working together without serious conflict. I'm inclined to believe that within a safe space to better understand oneself, an unforced, natural movement of unlearning and deep inner change is possible.

Parents were also joining us from a variety of economic and cultural backgrounds, some of them relocating from other parts of the country or even from abroad. There was a whole rainbow-like spectrum of enthusiasms and inputs, as well as disgruntlements. Some parents took to the place like a fish to water, and others grew to appreciate it and work with it. Some took what they could, gave when they were able, and then left for other educational establishments promising better things (sometimes with good reason). Parents were also invited to work together with 'what is', rather than what 'should be', and without losing sight of the necessary practical application of looking after their child's needs both in the home and school environment.

Working with the 'what is' of a child's temperament and their sometimes-entangled behavioural responses to their dramas and dilemmas, was somewhat easier for those on the ground than for the less present parents. In our small setting, diverse in activities, staff got to witness each child in all manner of situations: when Liam blew his top and pushed over Mac impulsively but then on another day invited him to sit next to him during circle time; when Kai put food dye in the toilet cistern or waved a butter knife at Ava, then later apologised (and giggled) for his successful larkish feat; when Sophi scribbled on Dora's drawing then ran tearful and remorseful to a quiet corner. We could see (sometimes instinctively) when menaces were actually pranks gone awry and reactions were mostly impulses on their journey to becoming better understood and self-regulated by the maturing mind.

Some parents were understandably wary and suspicious about such influences on *their* precious child, or of the potential pain inflicted by another youngster's misdemeanours. However, it was easier for the staff to tap into the compassionate place of acceptance and trust because we saw all the foibles and qualities revealed in the course of a week, or indeed a day, in our multipurpose setting. In our eyes, these children were not demons or future criminals, and they were rarely wanting to cause and sustain harm. They were alive beings who felt life deeply and strongly and expressed this in not always the most convenient of ways. Helping each other see the whole child required sensitive and thoughtful conversations between staff and parents as we navigated our differing views and perspectives.

There were many discussions to address all kinds of issues, not just related to behaviour but also learning. Sometimes, a common thread for a particular issue could be found, and steps were taken to rectify this for individuals or for school-wide purposes. At other times, what appeared negative for one person was something positive for another. More *direction* from teachers was asked for by some parents, while, in contrast, others wanted more *autonomy* for their child. Some valued free play beyond any other kind of learning; others wanted their child to be engaged in more specific study topics decided on by teachers.

How does one engage with differences of opinions (and possible underlying prejudices) without becoming entrenched in opposition? Creating a place in which all values and beliefs are pre-packaged and imposed has been tried in many cultures and historical periods, mostly resulting in institutional reasoning, ideological thinking, or cultish behaviour, thus inhibiting the seeing of things for oneself rather than through the eyes of another. Perhaps a vital aspect of any organisation is the extent of its sincere interest in the truth of things. Enquiring rather than convincing, thinking logically together and with humility of heart and mind allows the possibility for a shared understanding to arise, uncovering something that has a significance not attributed to a particular person or group's ideas.

•

Embracing the ethos of Inwoods as a full-time employee meant asking the same crucial questions even outside of the usual physical setting. That is, in working with 'what is' many of us saw the need to drop the idea of a work-life balance in which 'work' and 'life' are conventionally and conveniently divided, in favour of a more intuitive, integrated approach that also considered family members and their circumstances. Not all partners of teachers could be proportionately involved, but their input, whether in person or in spirit, was enthusiastically welcomed. And, sometimes, undeniably needed.

Loic was a parent, a teacher, a caretaker. He was the father of my sons, the homemaker, the family's pillar of presence and creative thought. He was (and is) my friend, my life partner, the person that never ceases to make me laugh and who listened to many of the struggles and issues that arose within the complex ecosystem of Inwoods Small School. In the early years, he volunteered to make the school site larger by transforming a whole acre of weeds and long grasses into a spacious sports field with a tyre play-feature. He designed a labyrinth and built an earth-oven, and himself led many work-parties that ignited philosophical chats while parents and staff were digging, weeding, and slowly enhancing the lovely woodland glade together.

Loic was not an admin fan although he *was* a fan of all admin-related devices. He worked hard behind the scenes to set up the much needed and expected technical infrastructure for communication within the school and beyond. He created a school email account, designed leaflets and flyers, mentored me with spreadsheets, forms and the Internet – until I could master them myself. Our characters and skill-sets are wide apart, but rarely are we in opposition to each other. I believe this was essential for the work-life integration, in which the working day blurred with evenings, weekdays became intertwined with weekends, and family excursions became inspirations for school trips and visits. Inwoods, our house, Brockwood Park, and the local surroundings became our home. Parents, children and staff became our family. Education became our passion.

Making daisy chains in the back field and learning the game "He loves me, he loves me not" but getting bored halfway round the flower

· 6 ·

Two Schools, One Vision

Brockwood Park School was founded in 1969 by J.Krishnamurti as a residential school for teenagers. Thirty years later, under the umbrella of the same Trust came Inwoods, situated at about ten minutes walk from Brockwood's main campus and functioning more or less separately, due to its younger cohort of daytime attendees and its greater parent involvement. Any collaboration between the two places arose mainly in organic ways out of interest from personnel when there were opportunities for an exchange, or when teenage students requested to spend time with the younger children as part of their studies and interests. As a result, a few interesting encounters took place between the age groups demonstrating what more could be done in our joint organisations if there is clarity and energy for solid mutual action.

Both Inwoods Small School and Brockwood Park School had Krishnamurti's vision at the core of their intentions, one aspect being to create the right climate so that the child may develop fully as a complete human being. Unlike many pedagogues, Krishnamurti didn't explain *how*, *when,* or *what* to teach. He didn't define any curriculum or lay out techniques. If he had, his schools would surely have fallen into the trap, like many institutions, of creating a system out of his words for schools to adopt and a child to fit in to. The emphasis would have been on the 'idea' of a *right* (and gradually becoming dogmatic) education model rather than on working together to have a greater depth of understanding into who each child is and what might be necessary for them, given all the circumstances of their being. Relationship, which all life hinges upon – and so, therefore, must education – is, by its nature, rather a creative improvisation and a living state of attention that no method can ever produce.

Brockwood's teachers were mostly residential with various roles and responsibilities spanning a full-length day. Most of the Inwoods' teachers lived within a twenty-mile radius, and in addition to teaching they were tasked with multiple duties intensely packed not only into the school day with the children but also often late into the afternoons with meetings and planning. Inwoods, at its height, had between 35-40 children on two acres of land, while Brockwood had 60-70 students on nearly forty acres that included a tennis court, swimming pool, art facilities, science labs, and its 'crown jewels': a beautiful grove of redwoods, azaleas and rhododendrons.

The distinctive nature of each of the schools, especially in terms of pupil ages, numbers, space, facilities and degree of parental involvement, inevitably created differences in the daily routines and opportunities of the two places. However, though set apart on two campuses, both schools attracted staff who were interested in the writings and philosophical questions of life that the Trust's founder raised. Despite the practical and functional differences, there were many similarities that included the caring approach to teaching and learning, and the community spirit that permeated each of the sites. In fact, from my perspective, I felt we were one place, not two, one main vision, not several, and both sites had the fundamental task of working together with others with sensitivity, sanity, and synergy.

After their time at Inwoods and their middle school years elsewhere, our adolescent boys became full-time students at Brockwood, enrolled back-to-back for a period of ten years. We lived at the gates to the school with an entrance onto the grounds of Brockwood from our back garden and an exit through the front door towards Inwoods, just a ten-minute walk away. Our home was adjoining a direct and obvious route between the two communities and was an occasional overspill station for visits and sleepovers for some who required it. I often worked in the evenings in the shared offices of Brockwood, preparing my curriculum offerings and catching up on admin-related tasks. This allowed me to connect with some of the Brockwood folk and experience the mellow hubbub of activity and student life, or the study hall's quiet, studious atmosphere.

Though primarily set up as *schools*, both places recognised the fundamental importance of engendering a healthy *community*. Learning how to function intelligently together requires a sustained attention to our behaviour in relation to others. As a boarding and adult residential educational community, people living at Brockwood ate meals together, shared the chores of keeping the place clean and tidy, as well as the joys of playing and interacting with one another throughout the day and evenings. At Inwoods, parents hung about chatting with each other at the end of the day – unable to prise their children away from their play on the now familiar and inviting grounds. Parents also assisted with keeping the place tidy, initiating work parties and preparing for the Autumn, Spring and Summer celebrations. These Inwoods' events welcomed prospective families, relatives, friends, Brockwood folk, and indeed anyone interested in the place. They were intended as fully inclusive gatherings out of which relationships and a cooperative spirit could be nurtured and encouraged.

The Inwoods' community arose from an unimposed inclination to function together and contribute to the life and development of this little school, whether for one's own child or a future child from another family. While there were guidelines in place regarding how one could help, and a request to refrain from meat-eating, alcohol, and smoking on the premises, the community of both schools was not built around strict social ideals or regulations. In this sense, they were not 'intentional' communities. Rather, they were schools inviting us to be mindful of our relationship to everything and everyone. They were inviting us to see where self-interest separates us into individuals, and if, in the absence of separation, we can arrive at real communion.

Despite this fairly liberal starting-point, Inwoods was not a laissez-faire place with people left to impose their views on others. Within a basic atmosphere of respectful conduct, everyone was invited to learn about themselves in the 'mirror of their relationships' (a phrase and imagery borrowed from Krishnamurti's teachings), which naturally meant showing up, joining in and generally coming together with others when school events and other opportunities were offered. The community at Inwoods evolved, changed and adapted from year to year, depending on who the cohort of parents, children and staff were at the time, for each person contributed both 'who' and 'what' they were to the group. Enough people were coming and going to prevent stagnation of creative input or an unintentionally exclusive culture.

Admittedly there was also the desire among some of us for less movement and more consistency of people and processes. We wanted people to stay longer, especially those who embraced diversity and aimed to communicate in straightforward and honest ways. There was the temptation to repeat what 'worked before' in terms of successful events, and discard what did not work. However, over the years, I learnt that a lot of what was 'successful' or what was not in terms of community happenings had less to do with structures and procedures and more to do with the degree of shared interest and creative input involved. While efficient systems are something desirable and no doubt necessary at times, there is nothing duller than having to take on someone *else's* well-crafted spreadsheet or lists and follow the laid-out instructions. Spreadsheets and lists are useful, but then there needs to be the freedom to bring one's creative input and a fresh eye to a task and thereby have the opportunity to learn something in the process. The natural transition of people also brought that new input.

If the culture we are in is not judgmental and critical, then we are more inclined to bravely join in, give something a go, and feel connected to a significant cause. Collaboration is so utterly essential in this complex world, where local cultures must confront global issues for saner technological progress and greater environmental care. If we as adults practise and model consultative and collaborative behaviour, maybe the children around us will pick up these vital skills for our planet's future well-being.

In the early years of Inwoods' growth, it lacked resources and staff. However, practically on its doorstep was a vibrant place with an international mix of people to draw from and items to borrow. Some residential Brockwood teachers offered classes at Inwoods in mathematics, pottery, drama and science where their schedules permitted this. Their input happened on a volunteer basis and was much appreciated but could not be regularised largely due to the competing demands on their time. I also saw the need for a less compartmentalised approach to teaching than one in which children are scheduled into subject-based learning with different subject-based teachers, something which, in my view, makes it more of a challenge for a deeper relationship to form between the young child, the adult and the learning.

However, I believed these early exchanges established a healthy precedent towards a spirit of sharing and collaboration as educators. We were far more than just neighbours. Arising out of a natural exchange at the dinner table, a passing comment in the school corridor, or sharing notes when staff worked alongside each other in the staff office, a few consistent and important initiatives were organised.

For instance, Brockwood's teacher of Care for the Earth (a mix of gardening and environmental awareness) had a regular weekly session with the children at Inwoods for several years, establishing excellent contact with them. There was no doubt that she loved her engagements with these much younger learners, and when the opportunity presented itself, I would love watching her. She had a soft voice and an untiringly tender way of responding to the children's energy and input that aptly matched the enduring tenderness with which she cared for campus plants. Sometimes she brought one of her teenage students to assist her at Inwoods, and for one term, she joined both age-groups for combined gardening and ecology-related sessions at Brockwood, with everyone benefiting in more ways than had been initially intended.

For many years we were fortunate to have the use of Brockwood's spacious hexagonal hall, one hour a week, for dance, movement and theatre-work, which also became the venue for some of our recurring annual school performances. There was also use of the school's pottery studio for two terms once a week, and of the arboretum-like Grove for visits in Spring when it was magnificently in bloom. Occasionally we used the tennis-courts for ballgames and other hard-surface sports activities that were not possible on the all-green-grounds of the Inwoods site. These minimally shared facilities (dependent on the approval of Brockwood's director at the time) were greatly appreciated, and instrumental in providing the broader curriculum we wanted for the children.

•

The institutional set-up of most schools promotes an *artificial* segregation of age-groups. Against their more natural inclinations, children are divided by class year-groups and separated by buildings into age-bands. It is no wonder that the young find it challenging to relate with others beyond their peer group, becoming entrenched in an identification to their same-age peers, and subsequently forming gangs and ranks that set themselves even further apart. One of the roles of an educator is to find ways to break down those walls that society has built and allow for the richness of relationships to emerge when interacting across all ages and maturity phases is permitted and encouraged. Within a healthy environment, the young freely take inspiration from those older than themselves. In turn, those older, more worldly characters, sense a new responsibility in their presence, rising to more sensible and approachable comportments as a consequence. There were just a few occasions at Brockwood and Inwoods when something like this did indeed flower due to the merging of their respective student worlds, as the following account illustrates.

In the Summer of 2015, Brockwood Mature Student, Miriam, who had previously accompanied us on a residential school trip, thought it would be a beneficially inclusive and fun idea to organise a joint 'sports day' for Brockwood students and the Inwoods children. Miriam checked out the general level of interest, got the go-ahead from the co-directors at the time, and coordinated a fabulous morning of cooperative games and team sports that involved all ages. It was the first time the two schools merged their student worlds and engaged playfully on something creative together.

One of the games over at Brockwood was a friendly football match on the South Lawn. The football that the children played over at Inwoods sometimes became overly competitive and ended in upsets if some groups were left to play unsupervised. When asked to share what they noticed when playing with the teenagers, the children responded with the following comments: "they talked to each other, telling each other where they were on the field"; "they gave suggestions instead of ordering like let's do the zig-zag"; "they spread out on the field"; "they had fun"; "they watched the ball all the time"; "they didn't get mad at each other".

Darshana shared the feedback she received from the children to a couple of the students who played earlier with them. One of them, Antony, mentioned how he had learned to play football only from playing with children older than him. He also commented on young Robert, who kept falling and picking himself up, playing with a determination and energy that was different from the other children. "Robert has a tough time in life", he remarked, adding other observations on the way Robert played, and surprisingly accurate deductions about his overall interactions with others and the challenges he faced. "I was like Robert", he stated and began to open up with his friends about his childhood.

Robert did have a tough time in life. His friendships were often fraught with aggressive undertones, his obstinacy in particular circumstances could drive him to isolate himself away from opportunities, and relationships were rough at home. I later heard that according to some, for a while Antony had not integrated as well as hoped with the environment at Brockwood; turning up late to classes and not attending important meetings. I wondered if his behaviour had not gelled well with the people and environment he had been raised in as a young child, and now he was reflecting on how this was impacting him as an adolescent.

Shortly after the whole-school event involving Inwoods and Brockwood, we had a surprise visit from Antony at Inwoods on a Saturday morning while staff and parents happened to be meeting in the sunlit strawbale classroom. He stood at the entrance, the glass doors wide open onto the deck where some of the parents' children were playing. He held two large boxes of 'Kapla' and explained that this was something he played with and loved as a child and that he was gifting it to Inwoods, having been touched by his interactions with the children over at Brockwood that day. Kapla is a simple wooden construction toy for all ages that stimulates spatial awareness and creativity; it became so popular among all the children that we set up a dedicated space for it for a time. No doubt there were other benefits that arose out of this rare mixing of students. Antony's story was certainly one of them.

·

Inspection visits for both schools were a regular occurrence and a statutory requirement for UK schools. It was the one time every few years in which 'all hands were on deck' in an unusually heightened feeling of *camaraderie* between the schools' administrative bodies and directors to be well prepared for the occasion. The outcome would be one report for both schools, so the evaluation of one would affect the other's result. In preparation for these inspections, we had to 'work together'. And we did. Meetings were scheduled, action lists created, and policy updating shared between the different departments. In the latter years, the countdown to the inspectors' arrival was run like a tight ship, and when they arrived, it was all handshakes, smiles and cups of tea.

But not only that. In the compliance inspection visit of Spring 2019, the inspection team was divided between Brockwood and Inwoods. A tall, suited gentleman was the first to spend the day with us. With polished shoes and an air of superiority, he arrived at the meeting point under the old oak on the edge of the sheep field where we greeted the children each morning. I explained to him that we were all on a first-name basis here and asked how he would like me to introduce him. His first encounter with the children was the countryside 'walking bus' from Brockwood to Inwoods with a group of playful children freely running ahead on the parkland and unmade track, stopping to stroke the horses, admire the bluebells and circle up before our quiet stretch to the gates of the school.

We were fortunate to have a glorious sunny day. As we didn't have a large enough office to fit several people comfortably, we made the picnic-table in the playground the inspector's station for examining documents and interviewing staff. While positioned there, he had a full view of the comings and goings and interactions of the children throughout the day as they moved between their learning spaces and playtime activities, a few of them without socks and shoes. Some children were oblivious to the hub of adult conversation, while others were curious, and would join in with their questions and outspoken comments. As the day advanced, I watched the inspector's demeanour progressively soften and relax amidst this picturesque and informal setting, in which both children and staff approached him *as themselves*. There were plenty of smiles and laughter, and by the end of that Spring day, he walked back to Brockwood with a distinct spring in his step to report to the rest of his team – not quite shoeless, but nearly.

Krishnamurti asked whether it is possible to think and work together 'per se', not just around a specific project. That is, not simply to work toward a goal in mind, or for a concept or around an individual's ideals, because such things eventually end, are limited and prone to conflict. Rather, to come together without a mind pre-set with ideas and opinions, and to think afresh, allowing a joint action to arise out of a shared understanding of what is necessary.

Getting through an inspection visit that laid out all the frequently uninspiring particular requirements – in a practically tick-box format – was a very specific task. There were few negotiations to be had because the whole aim of the exercise was to achieve an *expected* outcome outlined by legally binding regulations. It required a working team to get it done, though there were enough structures to hold onto, personal incentives, and clear consequences for the whole organisation if we did not cooperate. At the end of the operation, there was plenty of back-patting to fuel the storage of positive memories needed for the next inspection, and then the two schools went tiredly back to their separate functioning ways. Mission accomplished, driven by the eagerness to please the authorities, perhaps another important focus of our energies was wasted: that being to intentionally refine together our work with different age-groups.

During those well-defined inspection operations, I got a sense of the comradeship and collaboration possible between the two schools if there was a shared intention and clear vision. But intentions can shift, and, especially, they can range in depth and breadth from one person to the next. Vision, more often than not, stems from limited *individual* viewpoints that can be difficult to define, and problematic when groups try to align themselves without much questioning. Working together, not just around a specific project, means relating to each other primarily without having in mind our personal advantages and opinions. Is it not the work of our schools to transcend the narrowness of self-interest, avoid getting lost in the day-to-day decisions and projects, and instead think together about how to address the greater challenges that today's world presents to education?

•

Krishnamurti's writing is rich with insights and wisdom about life. Every paragraph can provide a nourishing meal to digest and reflect on before the next. One cannot read his books in a few hours or listen to his talks while engaged in something else. The language is simple, but the message is profound, appearing at times to be just at one's fingertips and at other times on far, uncharted lands. Both the rational and other more subtle insights were layered in his work, needing a quiet inner place from which to look and comprehend. He did not see himself as a *guru* and told people not to follow him or anyone else. "Find out!", he often said, *"What is far more important is to learn from the book of the story of yourself because you are all mankind. To read that book is the art of learning. [. . .] The book is the very centre of your being, and the learning is to read that book with exquisite care."* (From *'The Whole Movement of Life is Learning'*)

That book, which cannot be found on any school shelf, nor in any teacher's 'bag of resources', is nevertheless accessible to all of us who have the patience and attention to read its pages. Besides imparting necessary knowledge and skills, is it not a fundamental role of the educator to gently guide the children to find the book within themselves?

Learning about woodcraft and specifically red squirrels from Spinney Hollow's visits

· 7 ·

The Role of the Educator – Part 1

(Informal, non-formal and formal learning)

Here I am with my teacher title, ready for a new school day. Teacher, educator, facilitator, guide… call it what you like as the name has little significance. What is significant? Why am I here at the entrance to the school gate – or the Learning Centre – or the tutor room – or on a home-school mission with my child? Suppose I am here only to pay the bills, or bolster the school's reputation, or ensure my child gets to the best university. In that case, I will be doing a great disservice to this generation of children, who not only have the immense challenge ahead to cope with the complex demands of living, but also need to be prepared for a fast-changing world in which there is little physical or psychological security, no matter their grades or their certifications.

These children beside me do not know what the future will offer and have no historical perspective from which to get a clue. Their world is their immediate surroundings.

Their surroundings are the objects at hand and the people they have immediate contact with. Their world is the sky, the trees, the park, the road, the home, the friendships and folk that come their way. Children are not relating to a distant future predicament or a remote past occurrence; they predominantly relate to everything in their *present* circumstances in order to make easier sense of their environment and themselves within it. If this is the case, then what is my real and actual relationship with that child who has been entrusted to me by blood or bond? How will I help him or her to relate well, understand himself or herself, and to have the necessary capacities to journey independently and intelligently through an unpredictable life? The relationship between the educator and the child is what all of education hinges upon.

Lia holds my hand, and we both stand under the big old oak in our wellies and waterproofs on a sunny but crisp early winter day. Her hand is still warm from the morning's car journey to this school drop-off point. "Shall we put our gloves on?" I suggest, "Otherwise, we are going to have really cold hands by the time we get to Inwoods." I help her with her waterproof mittens, securing the Velcro strap to ensure icy water doesn't infiltrate and then put on my gloves too. Hugo suddenly appears at our side, "Mary-Ann, can we check if the trough has ice in it today?" he asks excitedly. "Sure, but remember to go along the edge of the field as the farmer doesn't like us to run across." "Yeah, yeah," he says, running off to hoist himself up next to Ted, who is straddled across the oak's long, low-lying branch. Lia sees her friend Annie pass through the gate and lets go of my hand to go and greet her. Eliot rushes past me, sneakily grabbing my hat on his way. A chase begins: around the trunk, in and around chatting parents, up to the fence and back as my hat gets passed between a growing number of playful girls and boys until I am out of breath and humorously pleading for its return. "Okay everyone, let's head off to Inwoods", Sam calls out. Children pick up their bags and follow him up the parkland while I wait to take the last child's hand, forming the rear end of this daily 'walking bus' to school.

The school's website stated that: *"The curriculum is not a set of externally specified, separate targets to be uniformly imposed upon the children, so much as a generalised lesson plan that in practice is adapted continually to meet the needs of the time, the school and the individual child".* This was a fairly close description of how teachers approached many of their sessions with the children, especially in the early years, when there were few resources to offer children free access to more independent learning initiatives. The educator can be an essential resource too, provided one is interested in the subject and is not constrained by technique, or enthused chiefly by the idea of needing to appear an expert. An 'expert' risks intimidating the learner unintentionally, turning the process into a guru-and-follower relationship, in which the one who 'knows' points the way, and the student imitates and repeats the methods to get there, resulting in a mechanical undertaking for all those involved.

During my teacher-training, I was very sorry to see one of the most dedicated education students on the programme drop his studies because he felt his spelling was not good enough to work with children. I was aware of my own spelling challenges, but I hoped I would get around this issue somehow. And I did – with the help of the children.

In 2003 I needed to step in for a few weeks for one of the teachers who had been taking care of the oldest group's literacy programme. The children were writing stories, and we were collating tricky spellings on the board as they came up. I was stuck on one – and it wasn't the first – dithering about with the board-marker in my hand and reaching for the dictionary. This time one of the children noticed and exclaimed with surprise and an uninhibited assertion that I was the teacher and shouldn't I know how to spell! "Well", I responded, "I don't know all the words in the English language, and anyway, my job isn't to tell you everything I know; my role is *to help you find ways to learn stuff yourselves*". After further discussion, that group of children were incredibly attentive to all the words and sentences I put on the board, spotting errors and double-checking a lot – their dictionaries gaining a new lease of life beside them. Yes, my spelling wasn't of the usual expected standard, but the atmosphere during those sessions was more engaging and conducive to real learning – once I stopped pretending to teach, and they stopped pretending to learn.

•

Inwoods' evolution of its approach to teaching and learning was largely shaped by circumstances such as space, resources, and the teachers' skills and styles at any given time. However, there were also opportunities to experiment more deliberately with approaches that we felt would benefit many of the children coming our way. One such approach was the 'Open Classroom', which we attempted first in 2004 and then implemented more consistently in 2010 when we had sufficient resources and more helpers to support it.

Many educators talk of the teacher-led versus child-led learning environments and debate over which is the best approach for children. If you are a radical 'unschooler', you might believe that it is better to be totally hands-off and let the child initiate all of their learning. If you are part of a mainstream setup, in which the national curriculum sets the pace and content, you will likely be on the other end of the scale and have to direct all of the learning, even if you didn't want to. Inwoods was not at either end of this spectrum, *neither* was it aiming to be at some defined and fixed place in-between. The intention was to be observant and mindful of *each* child's needs, questions and suggestions at any point in *their* development, and to sensitively 'step in' or 'step back' accordingly. The Open Classroom was set up to address and respect the shifting needs and necessities for self-direction, gentle instruction and a whole range of undefined ways of learning made available when there was little adherence to a particular approach.

For both young and old, but especially for the growing child in its voyage of discovery, freedom from the dictates and impositions of *others,* but also from the burdens and pressure from one's *own* personal desires and attitudes, is essential for developing intelligence of the mind and body, and of one's own authentic relationship to all of life. I observed that the younger the child, the more they seemed to demonstrate the need for autonomy in their choice of activities. As they matured and had more experiences of life, they appreciated increased input from teachers and finding out what they knew or could offer while continuing to appeal for opportunities that supported independent thinking and action.

Why should a child be expected to read instead of draw, do mathematics rather than write, or stay sitting at a desk instead of stretching out on the floor? The Open Classroom offered an open-plan space, in which mixed-age children were given free rein of the resources on the shelves and the offerings on the tables, while the facilitators moved about, listening and assisting where needed. They could also be found stationed at a table or down on the carpet, mucking in with the children's investigations and initiating undertakings in various corners of the Big Barn multi-purpose space. Visitors entering the room would often comment on the pleasant buzz of children contentedly engaged in something *alone or with others*. Facilitators, however, were far from having a starry-eyed perspective of the atmosphere; they were working hard at keeping an objective eye and were themselves constantly *learning* how to keep alight the many little fires of learning.

There is no one exact *replicable* way to light a fire, because *each* lighting requires a fair bit of attention to the delicate task at hand. You carefully layer up a few necessary ingredients – the paper, sticks, firelighters, whatever kindling you choose – include a log or two (or add them a little later), strike the match and watch; subsequently you still need to tentatively adjust the components and then the required amount of oxygen to fuel the flames. Once kindled, you step back to leave physics and chemistry to do its magic. Supporting children's independent learning in the Open Classroom setting was like lighting little fires and keeping the flame of curiosity and questioning alight. One needed to sense what ingredients were needed, without imposing, smothering, or dismissing, and without looking for someone else to demonstrate how to do it. It required, above all, an unbiased relationship and interest to understand each child and fully engage with them.

However, some fires didn't even need someone else to light them, especially when it was predominantly related to the children's creative and social learning. Children often gravitated in pairs and groups to activities such as construction with the Kapla blocks, or drawing, or making paper aeroplanes, because of the interrelational opportunities that they provided. Unless you observed closely, you would only pick up on a very partial aspect of their social world. One morning, I sat close to a group of seven-and eight-year-old boys, observing and jotting down some of what I could see and hear take place over a period of about half an hour:

10.37: Benji exuberantly gets up from the Open Classroom circle-time that starts the morning, stands behind Hugo and affectionately puts his arms around his torso. 10.40: David and Ted are constructing something alongside each other on the carpet. Next to them, Hugo is making a pompom while Benji holds the end of Hugo's wool. The atmosphere is one of camaraderie and giggles. Benji throws the end of the wool onto Hugo several times. Aware of Hugo's highly tolerant temperament, I suggest tentatively to Benji that he check with Hugo that he is okay with the wool being continuously thrown at him. Both boys turn to look at me but don't say anything. 10.43: Benji throws the wool again at Hugo. Hugo asks Benji not to do it again. Benji stops. 10.48: Benji encourages Hugo to wind the wool faster onto the pompom wheel and then asks if he can have a go. Hugo gives Benji the wheel and starts constructing something with the Kapla. Benji continues focused and quiet, meditatively winding the wool onto the wheel for a few minutes, then states, "I could do this all day". 10.51: Benji asks Hugo to get some scissors for him. Hugo goes to get the scissors, mumbling jocularly that Benji treats him like a servant. 10.52: Ted whispers something into Benji's ear and then announces that he is making a booby-trap with the Kapla. The atmosphere shifts to excitement. 10.56: Benji finishes with the pompom wheel and continues elaborating on Hugo's Kapla creation while Hugo starts making another one. Benji and Hugo deliberately make the first one fall down. 10.58: Hugo shares that his grandad is dying in hospital and requests that his friends not joke about dying. 11.00: While Ted and David are collaborating on constructing a marble run, Benji says to Hugo, "Ted just said the 'D' word". Hugo repeats that his grandad is dying in the hospital. 11.05: Noe joins the group, and Benji warns him that Hugo doesn't like the 'D' word. Noe repeats the word dying several times, which receives a tolerant response of silly gestures from Hugo. I suggest to Hugo that he explain to Noe why he doesn't like that word right now. 11.08: Noe settles to collaborate with Hugo on his construction creation, and Hugo speaks more soberly with him about his grandad's predicament. Noe listens with attention and sympathy.

While the children were busy with their hands, they were simultaneously engaging in social discourse *and* feeling their way through the situations that their words gave rise to. Though I had initially intended to make myself as invisible as possible, it didn't feel authentic to be sitting so close, pretending not to be present when I was. I relaxed into playing a small part in their relational experimentations while observing meaningful informal learning take place as they developed their creations and navigated their friendships. They did not question my presence or appear bothered by it.

Purposeful individual plans were also in the minds of the children and facilitators during their Open Classroom sessions: to write or finish a story, to work on personal projects, to engage with the maths equipment, or help Vince make lunch etc. These could turn into a somewhat haphazard undertaking when the children's interests and ideas were being interrupted by the push-pull of the social dynamics happening around them. One of the tasks of the facilitator was to check in with those plans and interactions and help bring some attention to aspects of their inner nature: what was motivating them or hindering them, whether there were any emotions or thoughts that might be impacting or contributing to their actions within this shared space. I found questions to be far more productive in the long run than offering quick-fix solutions that were quite tempting (though sometimes necessary) to do. A solution to a fairness debate between two children could easily be resolved by one of several options stored up an adult's sleeve, but to get the children thinking about their predicament and coming up with their solutions or observations took more time and patience, especially when it was revealed that fairness was not even the issue but that there was something more fundamental at play.

The Open Classroom space was a non-formal setting, free of many restrictions that allowed for informal learning to take place. It gave scope for children to take ownership and responsibility for their learning, both in terms of their foundational skills and with regard to the emotions and thoughts that were driving or draining them. They were learning to identify what interested them, to find *their* techniques to progress, to manage their time, to teach each other, and cooperate and collaborate within a shared space. Children were learning to 'self-direct' but without the self dominating all of the directing. Facilitators contributed and guided when needed, and were learning how not to dominate either, without losing sight of their role to maintain a safe environment for everyone. Learning was inconsistent, unpredictable, messy. But because of this, in my opinion, it often made it a richly valuable and necessarily unmeasurable affair, certainly unmeasurable by the 'usual' standards of categorising or labelling educational activities.

This 'messy' Open Classroom learning space was a catalyst for establishing a non-authoritarian relationship between the adult and the child, which inevitably affected all the other happenings in and around the school day. Formal education, that is, 'learning' dominated by outward form or show, is the predominant approach of many learning institutions. The learners and teachers work within a particular framework of predictably known knowledge, with assessment, tests, and certifications, often guided or imposed by the government at some level. While Inwoods certainly took inspiration from the National Curriculum material and also from alternative methodologies, it chose not to impose any systematic approach that risked blinding us to the child's true nature and needs. However, we also saw the value of including focused learning intentions and content in the format of class *topics* (that we mostly designed ourselves) which the Open Classroom was less able to provide.

Seen in this light, topics were a part of the weekly curriculum for most of the children in some shape or form. As well as taking into consideration the children's expressed interests, this was an opportunity for a teacher to share his or her passions and to inspire learning in an area of study that was perceived as necessary or valuable to them. In particular, we introduced the nine-to-eleven-year-old group to themes about the world that had them reflecting on humankind's impact and responsibility to it: how food is produced and distributed; sources of energy and their implementation; how life began; a general history of the evolution of the planet and humans' impact on it; ecology and the interconnections of life. The teacher's privileged access to the internet and books, and their capacity to coordinate with institutions and professionals beyond the school boundary, gave the children a channel into a broader realm of knowledge and resources than their classroom spaces and school grounds would otherwise have.

•

Trips and visits to places further afield were an essential feature of our educational endeavours. In 2015, a generous donor from Malaysia put funds towards a fourteen-seater minibus. Suddenly, the children's learning opportunities were expanded as we became able to explore places previously restricted to the immediate locality and a single school day. Residential trips now offered exciting potential for everyone involved.

It is the Spring of 2015, and we are about to head off for our first residential adventure: one large tent, several boxes of food provisions, three adults, and a giggling bunch of ten excited children packed into a minibus. With the steering-wheel in my hands, I pause for a moment before turning on the ignition to look over my shoulder and take in the rows of beaming faces. It had taken several weeks of planning and discussing the days up ahead together to get to this point, right down to the last morsel of food for our return journey. We all had some idea of what to expect, some sense of what the days would contain and how they would unfold on Pat's small permaculture farm in Dorset. But there was so much we didn't know. And that not knowing was the most thrilling part of all.

Children benefit from being exposed to various learning situations that work the body, challenge the mind, awaken the senses and inspire compassionate spirits. However, with societal pressures to fit children into educational systems and employment establishments that emphasise up-to-date knowledge and skills, we become anxious as to whether our children can keep up with the trends. That anxiety expresses itself either at the expense of reducing their exposures or by trying to cram everything in. Unfortunately, both approaches risk the child feeling overstretched with expectations or lacking opportunities for more depth of experience.

Halfway to Dorset, we scramble out of the bus to stretch our legs and have lunch on a hilltop overlooking the sea. Bellies full and energy replenished, we then exuberantly run back down the steep grass slope to the bus for the last leg of our journey. Pat welcomes us proudly onto her humble, once impoverished piece of land, which is now a nourished and abundant natural environment, thanks to her making. In those few days together, we learn about the delights and challenges of growing one's food, and about how to build a compost unit from tyres. We have a day at the beach: gathering seashore treasures and taking a dip in the cold seawater. We all sleep in one big family tent, cook together in the outdoor kitchen, eat while sitting around the campfire, use compost loos for the first time, as well as an outdoor shower cleverly rigged up in the polytunnel. Living here is different. Not cosy. We are out of our comfort zones and building up our tolerance levels for cold, damp, hard ground, sawdust, slugs, smoke, and wet shoes.

Something else was also going on. Beyond the usual school 'enclosure', where specific patterns of behaviour are triggered by habit and routine, a freshness of interactions brought about new connections in these novel circumstances that included us all. I saw the children interact differently with each other; girls and boys mixing more, less comparing, more appreciation of each other's company, a greater ability to work stuff out between themselves. The lines between 'us' adults and 'them' children also blurred as we struck a more relaxed natural chord within this more natural setting of exchanges and care.

In the days leading up to our departure, Rose's mother, Diane, was anxious and hesitant about her upcoming daughter's absence from her bed at night. Rose was often anxious too, resulting in an eyelash-plucking tendency which we were very aware of. Diane told us that Rose doesn't sleep through most nights, often randomly screaming out for her. "It can be pretty alarming, piercing", she told us, worried that this behaviour would not only disturb all the campers but leave her daughter feeling embarrassed, ashamed, and bare of eyelashes on her return. But Rose wanted to come, and because of this, we were up for embracing her bravery. As it turned out, Rose didn't scream, wake up or show a peep of anxiety those three long nights. In that big tent with the little pods, each in our sleeping sacks with Rose tucked in head-to-toe between Darshana and me, we all shared stories, cracked jokes, and giggled our way to slumberland after a full and rich day outside.

Patterns of behaviour and habits can take a grip in any environment, including the home. But they can also be undone, loosened, released, and that same energy channelled into new learning. Rose reported to her mum that she had "an amazing time" (with a complete set of eyelashes to prove it), and Diane shared with us that it was a "rite of passage" for the whole family. Aura's mum told us that she came back beaming and with a greater sense of responsibility, as evidenced in her new initiatives around the home, making plans for meals and launching herself into cooking for her parents.

•

It is surprising how much can be included in a school week when there *aren't* drills, worksheets, and rigid study programmes. Afternoons brought a broad range of extracurricular activities for the children to trial or taste or commit to for a fuller experience: clay pots and clay creations, spring flower printing and lavender bags, the making of Christmas wreaths and origami stars or Chinese New Year dragons, and science toys and woodwork constructions. Board-games, ball games, skipping, sewing, stitching, knitting and tinkering, all arising out of spontaneous offerings, or relevance to a season, or from such materials as could be begged, borrowed or brought to our attention. The free flow of ideas and initiatives set the tone and magic for a participatory culture that perhaps a more consistent plan might have squashed.

The participatory culture of theatre work was also a strong component of our learning endeavours. Our performances were all-encompassing events requiring actors, actresses, dancers, singers, prop makers, script editors, lighting and sound technicians, costume designers, and of course the appreciative audience of parents, family members and local affiliates encouraging this whole-school venture. Everyone had a role and opportunity to shine in their chosen expression whether as a performer or in setting the stage. However, as well as the obvious individual skills developed in the process, here was an opportunity to visibly recognise the impact one has on the whole; how one's efforts can raise or lower overall standards. And that actually, 'shining' is not an individualistic affair because to 'look good' one needed to work at ensuring everyone else 'looked good' too.

So much is decided on *for* children in their primary years of schooling without involving them. Adults choose the activities, set the groups and manage the sessions with strategies (some dubious ones) to ensure that everyone is 'progressing' and 'engaging' somehow. We did that too in some ways. But it begs the question: do we always know better than the child what is right for them and in line with their interests? In the last few years of Inwoods we experimented with even more autonomy for the children. Afternoons became an assortment of offerings that children could pick and choose from, but which always included daily an artistic or craft theme, something sporty or movement-based, and a space for a quiet, uninterrupted personal exploration or happening called 'Solo Time'. A fourth or fifth slot was given to other initiatives – child-or adult-led – which often included drama, music, dance and 'tinker lab'. For one term a particular favourite was I.R.S.T.R.E.P. (Inwoods Repair Shop & Tinkering Room Educational Project!). But, surprisingly, 'Solo Time' was often the most popular afternoon choice of all.

Solo Time. There were only two agreements: to be quiet, and not to disturb anyone. Otherwise, you could do whatever you wanted, including doing 'nothing' if it suited you at that moment. When we first introduced this period at the beginning of the afternoon, activity sessions and their groups were set mainly by us adults (though with some amount of negotiating and requests from the children). A familiar tune on the recorder would mark the end of the lunch break, someone would call out "Solo Time", and then the children would drop their play willingly and run inside to settle themselves into their choice of task. It was surprising how quickly the overarching majority respected and maintained the quiet atmosphere, correcting each other if there was a disturbance of any sort. For the 'teacher' too it was a 'doddle' to supervise; no preparation and little expected of us. Indeed, it was a gift to have such a moment with the children during the day. The most challenging part was getting everyone to stop whatever they were doing to clean up and move on in time for the other sessions – so engrossed they were in their chosen tasks.

With such eagerness of the children to rush to this self-directed, uninstructed time, I began to wonder if the children were still feeling the imposition of adult decisions in their environment despite the Open Classroom opportunities several times a week. However, having witnessed them continue to choose and enjoy these solo periods, when afternoons became both child and adult offerings, I realised something else was drawing them to this quiet space. It was not the absence of adults deciding. It was the delicious one-time opportunity in the day to be at leisure, doing what they loved without any interruption, pressure, or social bother from each other. Finally, they could be alone.

There is something rather special about being alone in the presence of others, especially if they are your friends, classmates or family. I am alone right now writing these words. My teenage son is in one corner of the room on a task, Loic on another; all three of us quietly and respectfully engaged in what is important to us at this moment. I get to glance away from my screen at the window and notice the bluetits on the hanging feeder. I get to sit here in the company of those I love and write at my own pace, observe in my own time, reflect and wonder uninhibited. No one is telling me how to write, what to write or how fast to write. I am entirely free to think and ponder, stretch my legs when needed and return to my task when I want, while myself respecting the quietness that holds this precious atmosphere of leisure and freedom for us all.

During Solo Time, nobody looked over anyone's shoulder; there were no benchmarks or expectations, no comparisons or risks of an unpleasant remark (unintended or not), no one dominating, and no triggers to initiate impulsive behaviour. In the company of others, there was solitude, quiet, moments of focusing and moments of reflecting. It was a much-needed interval within the busy, bumbling, bustling school day.

Another favourite afternoon activity was 'The Play of Painting' – inspired by the educator Arno Stern. Picture the scene: a practically empty room approximately four by five metres in size; the walls covered with brown paper; in the centre of the room is a well-crafted, narrow, free-standing piece of furniture that holds eighteen paint pots of gorgeous colours; beside each of these pots are three of the highest quality paint brushes – one large, one medium, one small. There is nothing else in the room. This simply converted shed with its transparent corrugated roof brought sunlight and rain sounds to complement this already incredibly inviting studio space.

Children crossed the playground, went past the vegetable garden and into the large covered-porch at the entrance to the studio, where they were greeted one by one by the *practitioner* on arrival. They put on an apron and entered the studio, leading the practitioner to a chosen spot of wall where he or she pinned up a large sheet of paper at a comfortable standing height for the child, who then immediately got to work – or as some would say, to 'play'. The practitioner's role was to serve the child (or adult if applicable): if a drip of paint started to run down the paper, the painter would call out "drip", and the one doing the serving would dab it up with a cloth; if a specific colour were not available on the palette table it would be mixed on a little lid by request. Most importantly, the practitioner neither taught, commented, nor judged the traces and formations of the person whose hands were at work. They were neither artists, teachers, or therapists, and the space they held was not an art class or a therapy session, though the therapeutic quality of what took place there was evident for some.

Lenny arrived at Inwoods, aged seven, traumatised by school. He was highly sensitive to ridicule, and rebellious in the face of authority. He stood at the entrance to The Play of Painting studio, refusing to put on an apron, agitated and twitchy. "I don't know how to paint," he said. "I'm not doing that". There was nowhere to hide in this room. Everyone's work was visible and scrutable, though Lenny didn't know that no one here did any scrutinising. Children were politely reminded not to comment on each other's work, and by the time Lenny arrived at Inwoods, children did not say things such as: 'Ugh, yours is much better than mine!' Or, 'It looks stupid! Why did you plonk that brown blob in the middle?'. And neither were there teachers making evaluative remarks for all to note and compare. Lenny watched at the doorway or sat on a chair in the corner where he could soak in the calm and pleasant, uninhibited atmosphere in which there was no mockery or mandating whatsoever. Within a few sessions of observing and tiptoeing in and out of the space, Lenny was also creatively rediscovering himself through stroke and colour. Finally, he was free from outer stresses and those stifling inner tensions of comparison and self-criticism.

A day at Inwoods offered the children experiences of the formal and informal ways and means of learning. The educator's role was to foster an uninhibiting environment where children could embrace the more explicit and specific aspects of non-coercive instruction and the novelty of focusing without resistance, while also giving space for the intangible to flourish in those moments of self-direction, reflection, creativity and play. The non-formal learning of our trips, visits and hikes, though partially informed by our topics and nature studies, were woven into the term and helped blur the lines between 'school' and beyond. The idea was to present and support a rich range of learning modes, thus preparing the young for the variety and flexibility needed when continuing their education journey elsewhere.

How did Robin's education journey continue elsewhere? Robin arrived at Inwoods at age five and spent all his primary years there. Now eighteen and writing to me from university, here is his unedited take on the combined learning modes of Inwoods.

> *"I think, when considering my academic achievements, perhaps the best thing that Inwoods has done for me, is to ensure I didn't see learning as a task, a chore, something that I would just have to do because that's how society works – whether I liked it or not – but instead something that I was able to enjoy and look forward to. I feel that the small classes, casual setting, and the complete disregard of the mainstream teaching syllabus and methods, in favour of more enjoyable content and (I believe) effective methods, were certainly big parts of why I feel this way. Although I've spent all the time after Inwoods in mainstream education, I think that this initial mindset that I gained at Inwoods has stayed with me throughout and has helped me enjoy secondary school and College a lot more than I would have if I had not gone to Inwoods. This mindset and my approach to learning has definitely evolved as I've progressed through the different stages and started to learn more difficult topics – but Inwoods has certainly given me an incredible start on which I've been able to build. Without it... I have no idea where I'd be right now. But the fact that I'm writing this from Cambridge leaves no doubt that we got something right."*

Please note, the fact that Robin is writing from Cambridge is not why I have included his statement (getting children into prestigious universities was not our mission). I have included it because of the predominant view that children need a regimented academic head start for such an achievement. Maybe not. Maybe what is needed is an intact spark for learning alongside a personal drive to get there. One thing is clear, Robin's noncompetitive, non-coercive, and test-free multi-approached learning environment in his primary years didn't hold him back.

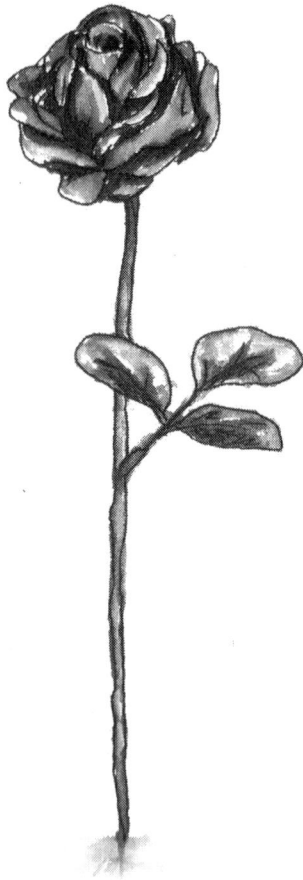

*Planting rose plants around Inwoods as our leavers gift to the school,
mine is on the side of the Small Barn within the raspberry bushes*

· 8 ·

The Role of the Educator – Part 2

(One-size-fits-all versus personalised)

The ability to read is probably one of the most crucial skills to have. It is the code that unlocks access to a wealth of knowledge. It is the way to find out how others see the world and to share in the pleasures of another's imagination. It is the route to greater independence, as signs, instructions, prescriptions, ingredients, notes, and messages become a more significant part of our maturing lives. Written language is indeed considered one of the pillars on which all ancient civilizations rested; without the ability to read, we would be lost in this modern civilisation too. A parent whose child has finally cracked the code and discovered this powerful tool for further learning, is visibly and undeniably relieved and excited by their child's newfound potential. No wonder schools make the ability to read at an early age one of their most fundamental aims.

However, learning to read comes with a whole host of complications and disasters if the process is not well integrated into the circumstances of the child's particular social environment and other crucial stages and aspects of their development. Large institutions that set the pace and implement one-size-fits-all frameworks for 'success', reportedly have many children plod along subserviently, developing dubious strategies to cope. Others are labelled and 'dealt with' for not keeping up, and a few, by hook or by crook, manage to evade the eyes of the prescribers altogether, and leave hardly able to read or write at all. The structure has little room for each child's uniqueness, and if they don't fit the system they are thrown into, they are likely to suffer in all manner of far-reaching ways.

The uniqueness of each child is an amalgamation of who they are when they enter this world, the behaviours they have adopted due to the socioeconomic circumstances they are born into, the level of care or degree of affection they receive, and their physical conditions and variable attitudes with respect to particular areas of their learning at a given time. Suppose little or none of this is taken into account. In that case, reading at the 'specific' age expected by the institution becomes sadly critical and potentially detrimental to the child's psychological well-being, as their 'intelligence' is put in question by those who compare and measure around them. But if this uniqueness *is* considered and there is no rigid framework to adhere to, then reading for each child can take its more natural course, and the environment can adapt and respond appropriately.

If there is a one-size-fits-all, failsafe tool out there somewhere to teach a child to read, I will not hesitate to take back what I am about to say. From my experience, there are numerous ways in which children learn to read, and at Inwoods we had to continually adapt our approach because what enthused one child didn't necessarily enthuse another. Undoubtedly there was also more than one factor at play. Some advanced happily with reading-scheme books, gobbling them up in their self-explanatory, systematic way: 1a, 1b, 1c, 2a, 2b... Some *randomly* picked out books from a loosely ability-grouped selection, jumping ahead and backtracking at their leisure. And there were those who sat with chapter books, analysing the words and decoding the sounds long before comprehension was possible – though this didn't matter to them because it was part of the fantasy and fun of what it might *look like* to be reading and that's what motivated them. That was how the reading-corner could be put into action in different ways and mostly through the children's own doing. There were also the little schemes of spelling-lists, word games, sentence puzzles and phonic worksheets that teachers brought in themselves so as to add variety and practice to the pot, not to mention the numerous books on display, and those times when children were read to, or when they read to each other. And in reading to each other there was a whole world of unquantifiable 'teaching' going on between these youngsters as they inspired each other and shared their tactics and techniques for progressing.

Some children seemed to teach themselves to read, *refusing any instruction*, while at the other end of the spectrum, others benefited immensely from some tutoring with a systematic approach for a certain period. We didn't have the resources to give such one-on-one sessions to all the children that we knew would benefit and enjoy it, so those few parents who were more financially resourced went elsewhere for this. Fortunately, most did this with little resentment, thus validating the mutual task of educating the child that we had entered into. Some children could read at age five, many took off around the age of seven, and a few grasped the skill seemingly quickly and suddenly in their later primary years. However, all were reading by the age of eleven.

Reading has its undeniable advantages, but it is perhaps also worth noting one or two of its drawbacks. Barely five-years-old, Sally was already an avid reader; she read in the car on the way to school and was often seen engrossed in a book beyond her years during her playtimes. In play, in her friendship interactions, she frequently appeared awkward. I wondered at times if she was retreating to books to compensate for her social discomforts, or if her reading talent was actually slowing down her opportunities to develop socially. Perhaps it was a combination of the two. One day, while all together in the Big Barn space, a storm suddenly arrived over the school with thunder crashing about our ears. All the children, except Sally, rushed out of the door to stand in the porch entrance and watch the downpour and incredible show of jagged flashing strikes across the dark sky. The excitement was palpable inside and out. Sally, on the other hand, was frightened, telling us how, in a book she had been reading, the story depicted a scene of lightning striking a child's home, causing the roof to collapse. Fantasy and reality were blurring for this little girl, so much so that she was unable to participate in the enjoyable thrill and be witness to an impressive natural phenomenon, despite our reassurances.

Zac, on the other hand, was one of the later readers and writers, but with an ability to remember facts and figures more than most. He loved his outdoor sessions on nature topics, eager to observe and notice what perhaps a well-crafted non-fiction, knowledge-imparting book might have robbed him of doing. Who needs to spend time finding out through observing if the information can be quickly obtained by the flick of a few pages (or the click of a mouse) where it says it all – and more? Who knows, maybe one downside of the cultural push for early reading capacity is the loss of those qualities needed to truly discover something for oneself. Direct observation and critical thinking are often what leads to innovations and breakthroughs. Very young children are having breakthroughs all the time as they discover what rolls, floats, sinks, breaks, falls, breathes, speaks, and many other wonders of matter, nature and language. But then something happens when textbooks, lectures and 'being told' take priority in their discoveries of the world; the child is no longer the principal actor and discoverer of their learning landscape but the follower of someone else's.

•

The official cut-off point for children attending Inwoods was eleven years old. This was when they would be expected to move on to secondary education; their parents would have the choice of large mainstream institutions in the area or private, expensive establishments. Few could afford the latter, and some chose to home-educate their child; but there were many who had to bite the bullet and hope that secondary school would be generous and gentle in integrating their freer-thinking, unmeasured child. Interestingly, many of the children who had completed most of their years at Inwoods looked forward to the change and the unknown challenge. They were excited by the prospect of more facilities and the opportunity to make new friends. With innocent confidence and the eager attitude to learning still intact, they were far from fearful. Their parents, on the other hand, were anxious and apprehensive, and they had good reason to be, especially if their child had only dipped into Inwoods for a few years rather than having had the uninterrupted and fully immersed experience of a more holistic approach.

Some parents joined Inwoods expecting their child to journey down a different education path yet arrive at the same destination. Others were more realistic about the potential outcomes, though secretly they also hoped that the route was only a 'detour' and would eventually meet up at the same arrival spot where all the other children in the neighbourhood, also aged eleven, would be standing – at the doors of secondary education and well-prepared for the expectations of the system. To be honest, that was my secret hope too, at least to begin with, until I realised that the meandering, slower-paced path of play, nature, creativity, art and craft, music and dance, personal projects and self-knowledge, was no match for the fast-track, ever-increasing speed of the straight and ambitious (predominantly academic) road to higher education. But this 'road' analogy is flawed anyway, because we weren't prescribing any arrival point (and certainly not one based on government requirements). We couldn't. Every child was unique, so there was no *one* road, *one* path, or *one* destination. There were multiple branches and offshoots. In fact, Inwoods was more like a tree, and we were mostly down at ground-level, devotedly making the soil around the solid trunk richer so that the various buds of all shapes and sizes could shoot out and blossom when the time for each of them individually was just right.

The how, when, and what of that blossoming in the child was an ongoing and underlying tension that permeated the place throughout the life of this little school. The fact was, at age eleven, children were going to have to leap into something else. And that 'something else' was not a continuation of the Inwoods environment. For many, it was going to be larger class-sizes, rows of desks, uniforms, marks and grades, behaviour reports, and strategies, all designed to keep the children in tow and in line with 'expectations' and 'projections' of a mechanised system. In the next chapter of their life, *comparison* was undoubtedly going to be a pervading source of insidious 'incentive' during the school day. All of us, teachers and parents (grandparents and relatives), were edgy and nervy as the children grew nearer to this unavoidable, age-eleven, cut-off point.

Remember Lizzie? The young girl who unabashedly pointed out to her teacher something factual about her behaviour back in chapter four? Lizzie had a straightforward relationship with her teachers, and her learning didn't stop at the school gate, nor was it left solely in the teachers' hands. There was a natural and fluid interface between home and school in which we all held her hand when needed and felt deeply responsible for her journey into life. As with many young school starters, Lizzie attended just a few days in the week, to begin with, and Mum hung about in the kitchen and garden as her daughter transitioned gradually into her independence from the home-setting. In those days, we got to know Mum as well as Lizzie. Not only was she there to build the bridge between home and school for her daughter, but she was also building bridges for us all.

Our relationship with Lizzie's parents grew and deepened as the months passed. This prevented artificial barriers forming between the educator and the parent, which can often become a cause of conflict within many settings. It was a straightforward and sincere relationship, not relying on sentiment and approval but grounded both in dialogue and in an unreactive unpicking of issues and possibilities. Much affection was also present, consistent throughout all of Lizzie's days with us and beyond. As I think now about this family, I'm reminded of the many such parental connections that were crucial to what sustained the challenging work at Inwoods over its twenty-odd years.

The challenges and tensions of the transition to secondary school were also present for Lizzie. At age ten years and three months, the heat was rising; choices had to be made, schools needed visiting, and Lizzie's readiness and academic potential required a thorough review in the context of her upcoming predicament. Lizzie appeared emotionally grounded, in touch with what she felt she needed, and valued for her comments and insights. Home learning was an option, but she instead pursued enrolment at a relatively small independent secondary school in a picturesque natural setting, which her parents were in the fortunate position of being able to afford.

Alas, this school required an entrance examination, which Lizzie knew about and was willing to prepare for. And so began the four-month countdown of the steps needed to pass, which included identifying what the exam would contain and any specific 'gaps' in her content knowledge, while becoming comfortable with test papers and grading for the very first time. It was an unbelievable marathon of a collaborative undertaking that included the parents, all the staff, and, most importantly, Lizzie's remarkable determination and resilience at every step of the way. To some extent it also included her friends and the rest of the Inwoods children, who had to respect Lizzie's focus and absence from some of their usual happenings with her as she worked hard to gather, practice and test the knowledge required for examination passing. And yes – she passed!

But Lizzie's story doesn't stop here. There is another flavour and noteworthy piece to this narrative that further demonstrates the complexity in the world of learning for many children when standards need to be met and there is a specific trajectory to follow. At Inwoods Lizzie was an eager learner, participating and enjoying most of what was offered to her with little resistance, though with some noticeable extra effort and time needed for spelling and reading tasks. While willing to engage with the additional work in preparation for her exam, the English papers were more of a hurdle for her, so her parents decided to investigate this with an Educational Psychologist. The results of an Assessment pointed out 'average' and 'above-average' cognitive faculties for particular areas, but with a measurement of 'below-average' in auditory short-term and working memory, particularly with phonological processing speed.

What I found interesting was the psychologist's comment regarding the unusually upbeat and emotional stability of Lizzie, in contrast to other children with similar discrepancies from mainstream settings, whose profiles depicted self-depreciation and a dampened relationship with their learning. At Inwoods, there were no yardsticks by which to compare oneself in the mixed setting of faculties and ages, and so there was less scope for a child's natural confidence to be knocked off course.

Possibly, if we had given eager Lizzie more exercises and extra support with her literacy progression from an earlier age, the exam preparation might have been less daunting for her. Though what would we have had to drop in order to accommodate this? And would she have been amenable to the drills at a younger age? I also discovered later that she was not the only one with so-called 'below-average' scores in certain areas. A few parents jumped on the bandwagon of Educational Psychologist Assessments (EPA) for a time, and a whole range of apparent 'shortcomings' were quantified: auditory processing; working memory; verbal comprehension; perceptual reasoning; processing speed; reading comprehension; mathematical reasoning; written language; oral language, to name a few. No child had the same score, though their reports generally identified that they were 'average' in most categories, had some 'advanced' aptitudes to their peers in other ones, and had at least one area less developed. Admittedly, I sometimes wondered why a child who seemed at ease with one activity (such as maths) was consistently not as at ease with something else – something as seemingly straightforward as listening to a story. Would an EPA identify that mathematical reasoning was strong, and auditory processing and maybe listening comprehension less so? But with or without these assessment reports, what is our response to these seemingly incongruous aspects of the youngsters in our care?

Conventional school-teachers have been known to tell children to simply 'work harder', while the less conventional sort have made comments on the need for a more positive 'growth mindset'. Either way, if the faculty is deemed as lacking in the context of testing parameters within which it is regarded as necessary, they are potentially doomed to be labelled by some as either lazy or too negative, and then probably dismissed by much of society as being not intelligent enough. This is quite crudely put, but sadly my personal experiences and observations of many children seem to fit this simplification, and life for these people can be a lonely place.

By contrast we might think of a few cases of physical impairment: someone with a shoulder injury attending a yoga class will be given alternative postures so as not to cause more harm; an asthmatic child will not be expected to exert herself in the same way in certain sports sessions; someone with lactose intolerance will readily be provided with an alternative meal. These people will be given the necessary amount of respect for their condition. They are unlikely to be seen as lacking in positive thoughts to fix their injury, too lazy to run, or unintelligent because their bodies react to milk. Unlike these *physical* conditions, so-called societal *cognitive* 'shortcomings' don't receive as kind or understanding a response. The label 'shortcomings', I hasten to add, is anyway only relevant within the specific context in which certain faculties are expected; otherwise, it's probably not a shortcoming at all, and the combined sensitivity of the teacher-parent relationship may discover untrodden pathways, including the option of apparently 'doing nothing'.

Is it possible to live, learn and work with each other with an absolute depth of respect and support for the other person, whatever the physical or cognitive expression at a particular time? No evaluations, no comparative judgements, and no hierarchy of faculties. What kind of world would that be?

•

Returning to the issue of the age eleven cut-off point at Year Six, I was surprised to discover the following. As several children would be transitioning to the local state system in the September of that year, I was delighted to welcome the Year Seven representative from one of the secondary schools in the area (TPS) to our little educational – far from perfect – haven. I was reassured to meet someone who seemed optimistic and unconcerned by the evident variety of skill sets and characters that would be coming his way. He told me that it was the same for all the children from the numerous primary schools in their catchment area. Each year TPS had to deal with the differences when the children arrived and would 'stream' them as they progressed through their secondary programme. So it seems, despite all primary school's dubious efforts to get children to the same place, it was mission impossible, and each secondary provision had its strategies for attempting to sort that out.

That year, the one child transitioning to TPS was found to be a couple of years 'ahead' of his peers in terms of his mathematical understanding, but he was lacking in some knowledge of the standardised topics that his peers had covered in their more institutionalised settings. Apparently, it never proved to be too much of a problem because he was motivated to find out what he needed to know to acquire the basics, and then 'caught up' with the rest as the themes took on more depth. This was common feedback about children who had spent a significant amount of time at Inwoods: an intact *interest* in learning, *their own* inner motivation, and *friendliness* towards adults and children alike – all of that supported their social and academic integration as much or more than any benchmark conformity. One parent's feedback, who had had two children attending Inwoods for seven years, suggested some improved subject content preparedness. But, he also stated: "If nothing were different, we'd still choose Inwoods and do it all again!"

Transitioning to secondary education was not a straightforward affair, and was largely dependent on how these schools embraced their newcomers *and* on the class teachers' particular values and stances. Expecting complete knowledge content and specific skills according to the measurable criteria of the national curriculum versus the unmeasurable values of curiosity and 'intrinsic motivation', could be a make-or-break situation for the child in their new environment. Stances varied from school to school, hence the parents' nervousness when that bridge had to be crossed.

Many of us dreamt of extending our provision to include a small eleven-plus programme. However, this was not an option according to the governors at the time, so we had to work with 'what is' and simultaneously be mindful of what would meet these children, while trying not to compromise on the fundamental requirements of an explorative and holistic education.[3]

---

3 Though Inwoods was not directly founded by Krishnamurti, as it was an initiative that took place 12 years after his passing, he had spoken of the importance of a Junior school at Brockwood to educate children before too much conditioning had happened. In a talk to students and staff of Brockwood in 1971, he is recorded saying: "They come here (referring to Brockwood) for two years, three years and are gone. It would be fine if they came here from the age of 5 till 18, then you could do something, but perhaps that may happen. I hope it will."

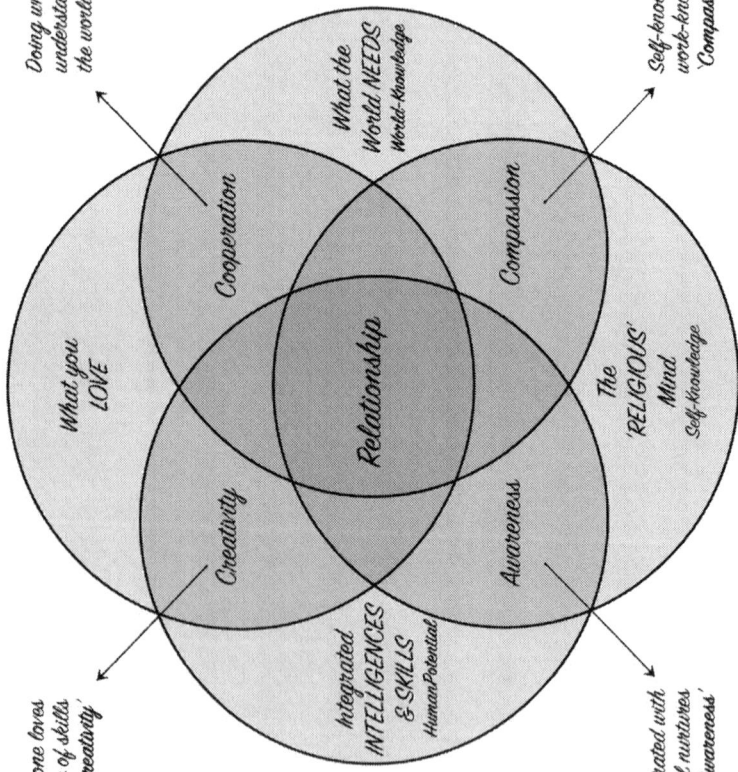

Doing what one loves combined with understanding our relationship to the world inspires 'Cooperation.'

Self-knowledge, integrated with world-knowledge allows for 'Compassion' to ignite

Doing what one loves incorporated with a range of skills is a recipe for 'Creativity.'

Self-knowledge, integrated with human potential nurtures 'Awareness.'

What the World NEEDS
World-Knowledge

Cooperation

Compassion

What you LOVE

Relationship

The 'RELIGIOUS' Mind
Self-Knowledge

Creativity

Awareness

Integrated INTELLIGENCES & SKILLS
Human Potential

· 9 ·

Holistic Education

Many alternative schools across the globe use the term 'Holistic Education' to describe an educational environment that integrates numerous fields of learning rather than the mere pursuit of academic trends or specialist skill sets. In 2018, following a visit to several alternative schools in Europe, I facilitated a review with some teachers and parents of this rather loosely bandied-about term. One outcome of this was the graphical representation on page 122, of a possible holistic approach (inspired by a Venn diagram of the Japanese concept of *'Ikigai'*). Our version depicted four petals signifying what was perceived as essential focal elements in a school setting. The intersections between these petals show the qualities arising from their combined effect.

'Integrated Intelligences and Skills' encompasses not only academic aptitudes but those that involve the body, hand/eye coordination, artistic flares, expressive art forms, teamwork and oracy. They require mental capacities and

social and emotional intelligence, and an awakening of the senses working together.

'*What you Love*' speaks for itself. When one truly loves what one does, one does it not for anyone else's approval but for the energy and joy that it brings. Incorporate doing what you love with a range of skills, and this is a recipe for 'Creativity' and the human potential to shine.

'*What the World Needs*': The world needs looking after in every respect, environmentally, socially, culturally, and politically. When we realise what is going on in the world and understand our relationship with it, we begin to care, and when there is care, we act. If in that action there is compassion and doing what one loves, 'Cooperation' emerges.

'*The Religious Mind*': not a mind that attaches itself to some dogma or fabricated spiritual story, but a movement of enquiry that is continuously attentive to the nature of the self and the inner workings of both the heart and mind in its factual relationship to nature and the world of humankind. Self-knowledge, integrated with world-knowledge and human potential, allows for 'Awareness' and 'Compassion' to ignite.

But what if we take one petal out of the four away? We can do what we love in the context of what the world needs, and while paying attention to our mind's inner workings, but without the development of integrated skills one is likely to be limited in effectiveness. Without doing what one loves, there may be a sense of contribution but a lack of joy and enthusiasm. Without world-knowledge and participating towards a better world, one may be prone to an individualistic livelihood. And finally, without a religious mind, life could feel fragmented and empty.

This graphical design was a creative way of capturing some fundamental principles of what could be considered a holistic educational setting, and a useful tool for considering how each petal might be translated into concrete actions on the ground. However, there is the temptation to create a packaged educational theory out of such diagrams despite its lack of relevance to practical circumstances, so we chose not to use it for anything else other than food for thought. In fact, in a brainstorming session with parents, we considered other petals, different overlapping qualities, and a whole range of happenings beyond what we were doing or could conceivably achieve. It was an essential inquiry into our roles as educators and parents, and an opportunity to review any expectations and assumptions that might be interfering with a freshness of insight regarding what was possible and vital for the children in our setting.

Some other ideals and expectations needed to be unpicked too, 'academic excellence' being one of them. At Inwoods, there was both reverence and wariness – across the teacher and parent body – in the face of this very loaded term. Krishnamurti spoke of it, it was the selling point for many schools, and indeed we had also put it somewhere on our website. Of course, everyone wanted their child to have the necessary 'academic' skills to function in this world, but what did this mean or look like on the ground in terms of 'excellence'? And how could we be clear as a community when there was such a mismatch of opinions as a result of personal experiences with the conventionally imposed formulas of assessment and grades?

•

The word 'academic' is often seen as synonymous with the theoretical and the conceptual, requiring instruction and training, and resulting in certificates and diplomas. It involves content, knowledge, facts, and the capacity to memorise and accumulate information or statements provided by others. We envisage gaining academic expertise as a result of intentionality and rigour. For many people who have been hurt and hindered by academic study, the above notions conjure up images of young children sitting in rows and being drilled, tested and certified for the knowledge that they have managed to regurgitate, from circumstances that are largely meaningless as being out of touch with their reality. The word 'excellence' suggests perfection, exceeding and succeeding over others. One thinks of medals and awards, being the first, the best, the highest, being superior to anyone else. 'Excellence' calls forth images of competitive environments and comparative thinking, not to mention an awful lot of anxiety. It is no wonder some people are rejecting these terms. However, is it possible to embrace the broader aspects of academic excellence rather than a result-oriented outlook focused on turning children into careerists?

Reaction and suspicion of 'academia' is likely to compound the divisive worlds of mainstream and alternative education and hinder a clearer understanding of what is needed for an intelligent relationship to learning and life. Academic excellence has its place if one does not define it within overly limiting terms or only consider certain subjects academic. At Inwoods, I witnessed children memorising poems and chunks of lines for their school plays and rigorously rehearsing with self-determination. I saw eager-eyed children following the instructions of how to make a basket and executing it with persistence and their own unique touch. Songs were taught, practised and presented with a quality of joyful collaboration and attention. Children thoughtfully watched the delivery of a science experiment that ignited explorative questions and hypotheses, and they worked through the tough patches of completing a piece of writing or illustration. There were mathematical equations to solve, and then facts to assimilate and include appropriately in personal projects without there being extrinsic motivating factors at play.

When children played and interacted at leisure, they were frequently seen critically thinking through their water-harvesting ideas and other play feature constructions. They required creativity and flexibility when inventing new games collaboratively or organising skits and dance pieces. They experienced how sustained observation led to enhanced understanding during their quiet moments in nature or during walks. From stillness emerged a heightened quality of attention, and coming to lunch on time necessitated an awareness and respect of others. With the opportunities for the children to make choices and reflect on their actions, a sense of responsibility was nurtured. This, in turn, taught them to discern wisely and grow in confidence to make important decisions. Academic excellence should not necessarily be linked to competitive environments, coercion, specialisation, the mere accumulation of facts, or the pursuits of specific outcomes. In reality, it is visible in a broad range of activities and encounters with life, and includes an extensive array of qualities that can flourish when greater freedom and responsibility exist.

But that alluring word 'Freedom' throws up just as many knotty issues as we find with 'academic' and 'excellence'. It is a word that seems to have multiple definitions depending on the context in which it is used: Freedom of speech; freedom from imprisonment; freedom from the power of another; freedom to move; freedom to do as one pleases. But what happens if my freedom impacts your freedom when I push for my words, interests, and actions to be expressed and fulfilled? And if I am influenced by the words and actions of others, or thrown into conflict by my reactions and contradictions, am I really free? These were some of the questions that we were grappling with in our education setting, where freedom from habitual behaviours and reinforced responses was understood as a vital element in the child's blossoming.

•

Conflictual incidents and clashes of personalities are an ongoing occurrence in the worlds of the children. But if one has the patience at the time, these are also opportunities to reach out to the unconscious aspects of the child and awaken their own intelligence. With holistic education in mind, here is an opportunity to attend to the self-knowledge of the child.

During one extended playtime, a group of children had been busily preparing a space for their cake-stall. Preparations had been underway for several days as they decided on recipes, allocated roles, created free purchase tickets for each child and adult, and baked in their homes. It was a child-led little enterprise that involved a fair bit of collaborative work and was about to come to fruition at the end of the school day with treats in store for everyone. Rowen, six-years-old, arrived on the scene with his ticket just as the older children finished furnishing the space, but they sent him away, explaining that they weren't open yet. Unfortunately, this was not how Rowen had understood it. He left feeling excluded from having any cake, angrily returning later, when the children were not about, to sabotage their notepads in revolt. After a bit of detective work undertaken by some children his misdeeds were uncovered.

Rowen was a spirited chap who couldn't stand any injustice, and most of the children were somewhat wary of his unpredictable outbursts when things weren't going his way. On this occasion, rather than try to sort the situation out themselves, they brought Rowen's actions to my attention. It was a delicate task as he appeared resentful and uneasy in the playground, and I wasn't sure if he would run off when I approached him. I hung around in his presence until he came naturally closer and then asked him how he was doing. I gently took both his hands in mine and, speaking softly, began acknowledging factually and without criticism how angry he was earlier with the children. With his nervous system calmed a little, he opened up about his actions, explaining his reasoning. "Are you sure they were excluding you from the cakes?" I asked. "No one has had any yet. It's at the end of the day when they will start serving," I slowly explained. "Do you have your ticket?" Rowen looked at his ticket and realised that he had indeed misunderstood. We were both quiet for a moment and then we reflected on the consequences of strong reactions and wants – mine included so as not to induce a feeling of diminishment by the incident. I asked him what could be done about the damage he had created, and he requested I help him with an apology note.

In the spirit of such exchanges, we attempted to address conflicts without reprimands, and to raise an awareness of the actions and thoughts that might be contributing to any disharmony in relationships. This required tireless work and an abundance of patience, and could not be formulated into a script of sorts because each child was a unique individual with their particular quirks and qualities and ways of connecting with us. There were also the impulses of young children, scientifically shown (I'm told) to be due to the natural development of the brain in which the prefrontal cortex is underdeveloped, and so no amount of rational discourse was going to change anything at that moment.

Some older children's reactions were based on hurts and troubles that couldn't easily be addressed through gentle chats, enquiry or mediation. Sometimes it meant removing responsibilities that could trigger further inappropriate or unpleasant consequences. For example, a child that had destroyed another child's sand creation for the third time after several attempts at problem-solving the issue together, would be led away from the sandpit or shadowed closely, depending on the staffing situation at the time. And depending on the spirit in which such incidents were handled, this form of action taken by an adult was either a natural consequence of particular behaviour or considered a form of punishment in disguise. Ultimately, our intention was to avoid communicating a feeling of condemnation, which was not always easy.

With no scripts to go by, a whole range of brains in their various developmental stages, the dynamics of personalities to contend with (as well as limitations in staffing at certain times) there was only one thing we were left with as adults in the face of each child's predicament: affection. On such occasions one might be emboldened enough to call this movement love, while recognising that this affection-love was not always there, and no amount of self-criticism or guilt-imposed feeling would change this in oneself. Working with 'what is' in our holistic setting also meant a conscious non-judgmental seeing of what was lacking in ourselves. This, in itself, created an important quality of community humility and potential for dialogue and growth.

Freedom, in the context of our educational approach, was not about doing *what-one-wants* but having space and leisure to freely observe one's desires *in the context of living with others*, and included the broader purpose of bringing about collective change. This was an invitation and a challenge both to the individual and to the community, and required eliminating anything that might create further barriers to developing the necessary attention for such work: there could therefore be no undermining, ridiculing, shaming, measuring, or comparing one child to another. It required conversations that were not 'preaching' and a presence grounded in *listening* rather than casually concluding. In essence, it required creating an atmosphere free of fear.

Holistic education can be seen as the integration of *all the petals of life*, the vital elements of both the inner and outer, the me and the you, what I do in my relationship with people and in the context of everything around me. Fragmentation happens when the parts are isolated from the whole or missing altogether. When there is attention to relationship in its truest, broadest, deepest sense, in the educational setting (rather than giving the greatest emphasis to mere knowledge and explanations), then learning becomes more immediate and meaningful. It is born out of an energy that has its own momentum for content, rather than a preconceived and adult-imposed curriculum-style concept. Ideas about how and when to 'step in' or 'step back' from the child's learning are dropped. Instead, we can walk side by side in an affectionate relationship of sharing, receiving, observing, questioning and listening, unhindered by the stale expertise or political bias of authorities or taken-as-given educational ideals. Perhaps then, the immeasurable flowering of an intelligent human being can happen, unforced, almost unexpectedly.

The group the 'Cherry Blossoms' along with
friends, teachers and locations associated with it

· 10 ·

Nature Education

Today is the last day of March, and the first morning I can fully open my window and let the sun's warmth and birdsong fill the room as I write these lines. The trees on the horizon are bright green with the first shoots of leaves, and the pear and apple blossom below are teeming with bees. It is spring at last, and a perfect moment to reflect on the place nature had in the lives of the children at Inwoods.

Every morning we immersed ourselves in nature as we leisurely made our way along the parkland, across the gravel track beside the woods and the horse-paddock, and then under the large mature trees that arched over the country lane to the school gate. There were iced-over puddles to touch and crack in Winter, bluebells to enjoy in Spring, horses to stroke, a favourite tree to scramble on, and the extraordinary detail and beauty of spider webs, dew drops, sunbeams, fungi and bird calls. Every day there was something familiar to encounter and something new to discover as we skipped, strolled, ran and paused to take in the many delights of the Hampshire countryside and its ecosystem through the seasons. This was the start of each school day.

It wasn't always a pleasant start. Sometimes a goodbye to a Mum was difficult, or there was an unkind word from a friend, or a competitive attitude to navigate at any point during the length of the walk. There were stinging cold toes to tolerate, a limping lamb to witness, or a dead bird that was first poked at, then mourned for, and finally buried or hidden in the leafy undergrowth. On some days, torrential rain soaked our faces and blurred our vision, calling for a mighty resilient spirit to help us collectively forge ahead to the shelter of the school barns.

As society becomes increasingly shaped by our attraction to the instant gratifications of consumerism and the pursuit of personal drives, we become progressively more disconnected from the natural world. The inevitable result of such self-centred actions is a diminishing sensitivity to nature and ignorance of the harm we are causing, both in terms of individual well-being and the environment. So, with this in mind, what role does education play?

Inwoods was fortunate to find itself evolving in an attractive rural location where the children could be exposed daily to the natural elements and to the fauna and flora of its surroundings. This environment readily set the culture for many happenings outdoors, which parents welcomed wholeheartedly from the moment they set foot on the grounds and enrolled their child. It was a perfect setting in which to witness the unfolding of the children's intrinsic interest in all things natural and their enjoyment of being in and surrounded by nature.

Throughout the years, there was always an emphasis on bringing into the school day moments of quietness and contemplation in whatever shape or form. Sometimes a session would start with a moment of quiet, or we would light a candle and attempt to bring stillness to our circles. Unsurprisingly, the classroom walls or the proximity of wriggly bodies and racing minds often interfered with these endeavours. Until, that is, we took ourselves outside for 'sit-spots' and let nature's sounds, sights and smells inspire a quality of silence and aloneness that many of us saw as crucial nourishment to the children's growth in sensitivity and attention.

From 2016, sit-spotting happened every morning for at least ten minutes, rain or shine, as soon as the children arrived at Inwoods off the 'walking bus'. Senses awakened, the gate would open, and we would all disperse in different directions across the playground to find a place to be, preferably a few metres away from anyone else. Children could be seen tucked within the low branches of a tree, on a log, sitting on top of the large tractor wheel play-feature or curled up inside it, below a bird box, with their feet in a puddle, lying on the grass, or facing the surrounding woods. All external human activity ceased so that our attention could be drawn to the circling birds of prey, cloud formations, insects, the wind or sun on our cheek and other natural sensations that grounded us in the reality and presence of nature's embrace. The guests and visitors who happened to join us for these sittings were themselves touched to have been included in this collective reverence for nature, and often shared their surprise at the children's capacity to embrace it daily.

It wasn't a forced practice but admittedly did require an element of 'upholding' to make it possible. Given complete freedom of choice, some children would likely have been tempted to spend the time socialising and playing instead, subsequently influencing others to do so. In the same way that a parent might respectfully assert the importance of coming to the table to eat, to bathe, brush one's teeth, prepare for sleep etc., we continuously discussed the value of this whole-school activity and the need for it to be a collective endeavour for it to work. But within that framework, children chose to sit where they liked, observe what they wanted, look outward or inward, and take notes or sketch. A few children sat close to an adult or a friend, and occasionally one or two waited inside for reasons quite specific to them.

To be alone and unstimulated by the constant actions of others and free of the triggers of the chattering mind is a challenge for us all. Sometimes I would sit in my spot completely absorbed and touched by the beauty and simplicity of this moment in which all of my deeds and drives ceased. At other times, I confess, I would be lost in thought, planning my next move, watching the time, or distracted by the fidgets of others around me. I imagined this must have been the same for all of us positioned in our little worlds on different days. And when my attention was drawn to my young companions, I noticed similar spells of slipping in and out of awareness and appreciation. There were mornings in which I doubted these efforts, and other days when a quality of peaceful respect and communion with nature wondrously permeated the whole school setting.

•

With very few exceptions, we human beings all arrive in this world eager to learn, and with wonderful capacities to observe, listen, and be alert with all our senses. In the formative years, there is very little judgement in our endeavours to understand our surroundings. Our interests are hardly selective; we are curious and open to whatever is in our pathway, unselfconscious of our potential. However, in the highly intellectually stimulating environment of most schools, where thought is considered a powerful tool, there is a shift from this sensorial, unambitious approach towards learning, to something that demands great verbal capacity, quick thinking, and the ability to measure one's 'progress' (or to have it measured by others) so that we can join the competitive path to 'success'.

At Inwoods, we made a conscious shift away from the quantifying and fast-paced educational approach to an environment that offered the child immersion in unmeasured and uninstructed periods in nature. In the course of each season, we took the whole school of children on full-day excursions to a local landscape. Some of the favourites were a yew forest, a chalk grassland, a bluebell wood, a deer park, a heathland, and a few places along the coast.

On such days, instead of heading off to Inwoods when we arrived at the usual oak-tree drop-off, we would circle up to identify who was with us, check provisions, allocate vehicles, introduce the day ahead, and remind everyone of our safety protocols. We were mostly a jolly bunch of kids and adults with backpacks and water bottles, caps or wellies, eager to head out for a whole day under the open sky. The occasional one or two anxious newcomers who boarded the bus with us, sometimes tearful despite being encouraged and supported, would always disembark with a cheer at the end of the day.

On most occasions we were fortunate to bring along someone who knew a lot about the area or the nature we were visiting. In the last four years, Toby was our walking nature encyclopaedia, and a passionate advocate for meaningful engagement with the outdoors. When Toby was with us, there was always something for everyone; an organism to smell, touch, taste or gaze at together with relevant information to marvel about. Whether you were four or forty-four, you were free to tune in and out of the most elaborate discourse on the complexity of an individual life form or of a whole ecosystem, or simply enjoy the physical sensations and modest facts that he brought to our attention.

The Deer Park was a yearly meandering amble in the grassy rolling landscape, dotted with fallow does and their impressive looking bucks. It was the chance to learn a few facts about the annual rut, listen to the mating calls, and observe the battling bucks. There were all types of animals to spot on our grassland trips, from the largest (roe deer) to some of the smallest but, in ecological hierarchy terms, some of the most important. We learnt about the yellow meadow ants that live in interconnected hummocky hills and carry chalk hill blue butterfly eggs, caterpillars and cocoons into their nest, where they protect them and milk them for honeydew poo until the adults emerge in the Summer. It was a glimpse at the wonderful examples of symbiosis in the natural world, something one would have no idea about unless you were with someone who knew, and you took the time to listen or to find out. The Heathlands' trek brought ferns, fungi, and mauve flowers to our attention, followed by an inevitable noisy scramble along fallen branches, quiet sit-spots among the bracken, and a picnic-lunch in the shade of the trees.

While the daily morning walk to school helped focus the awareness on details in nature within a particular and familiar environment, our longer excursions and hikes put those details in the context of a whole landscape. Landscapes vary and change with the season and climate, so there was a lot to discover throughout the year. Children's natural inclinations to move and expend energy meant that the connection with nature was primarily *physical*, as they eagerly wanted to find out what lay beyond the bends and hills of their paths. Along the way, they spotted trees to climb, rocks to scramble over, hills to roll down, and, if they were lucky, streams to paddle in.

For the novice young hikers, the landscape was more of an exciting 'playground' than anything else. Still, with time and guidance, they also discovered that it was alive with life and required sensitivity and care to navigate. Once they had found birds nesting in the trees that they climbed, they explored the branches with additional attention and care. Rocks, where insects had been found to hide, were no longer kicked and abandoned but carefully upturned and replaced. Thus, the playful physical explorations of nature's elements grew to become respectful investigations of landscapes, with a deepening understanding of one's relationship and responsibility within it. Darshana recounts:

> *"On one such excursion a child found a deer antler. These are dropped in the fall and eaten over the winter by the deer to reincorporate the nutrients, but that Spring, one such antler had remained and was discovered by keen observation. This discovery caused such ripples of admiration, jealousy and avarice that it was the topic of most of the day – some were tearful but most were reflective. On the walk back to the vans, a hovering observer would have eavesdropped on many a disclosure from one child to another or to an attentive adult about desire and disappointment, possessiveness, accepting one's feelings and yet letting go of them, the transience of life and the delights of really paying attention. One child commented that she hadn't found the antler but she had seen a flower closer than ever before and found that – a different kind of gift."*

We often had a few parents join us on these trips, as well as a guest or two. On one such occasion a university education student visiting for a few days spent the day with us at a nature reserve. On the bus journey heading back, she surprised me with her comment about her never (ever!) having had a whole day outside before. She described how well she felt and how inspired she was to see the children with such resilience and joy in what she felt was tough terrain for little feet. It struck me that perhaps many of this generation's young student teachers were not raised with much experience of the outdoors and therefore may not consider or perhaps feel comfortable incorporating nature education into their practice.

Is this nature deficiency, this increasingly shallow relationship with the nature around us, an inevitable result of the increase in time spent on social media platforms, and altogether the overall escalation in adult and child mobile usage? Will this trend adversely impact what is seen as necessary and vital in working towards a more sustainable world? Indeed, a lot of social networking has, by contrast, actually helped raise awareness of serious issues, and technological advances could have an important role to play in terms of attempted solutions. But without a deeper feeling and sense of care for the splendidly complex world of diverse species, what will be the motivating factor to protect and preserve it wholeheartedly?

Without a greater practical love for this planet, I see us heading, at worst, towards the destruction of most natural ecosystems on which our human societies depend, and at best, finding mere technological solutions to ensure humans have the essential minimum of clean water, air, and food, but at the expense of everything else. With our basic survival needs met and our virtual worlds enhanced and cherished, who needs tigers, elephants, ants, butterflies, seas brimming with life, and spectacular landscapes of all varieties? A gloomy prospect, to say the least, but perhaps, given more opportunities for an experience of a real and tangible communion with nature, one would never let this happen!

·

As well as our sit-spot mornings and our landscape excursions, there were also our nature day happenings that took place every Friday. Following the sit-spot time, children circled up to hear what was being scheduled, and then groups of children rotated around the three or four offerings throughout the morning. The two 'regulars' were gardening and/or grounds work, and ecology/bushcraft. Other sessions switched between observational nature drawing, local walks, making wreaths and lanterns, pond discoveries, and those other *seasonal* crafts and opportunities that the outdoor environment could offer. By the end of the year, most children had made at least one basket or mat, and had painstakingly whittled a spoon or a spatula. They knew what was edible among the flora of the school grounds and along the adjacent lanes. They could make elderflower cordial, identify animal tracks and scat, build shelters, and plant tree-saplings.

Over the years many children became budding gardeners. After much experience and consistent determination, Darshana had a way of transitioning a child from a hesitant attitude of loathing for earthy hands and hard work to a willing and industrious steward of growing and caring for plants, including the soil they were growing in. Her sessions would start with a story, and then evolve into small teams planting, weeding, watering, digging, chatting and giggling. "I am picturing a team of three to six children getting the giant gooseberry bush out of the garden bed because we wanted to move it to a new permaculture bed", she told me when reflecting on those days. She later wrote:

"A couple of children stayed, and many came and went as they dug up and rocked and freed the complicated root

system. Then their absolute delight when they got it out, and concern that it gets placed quickly in its new situation and watered and fed well."

Work parties on the grounds were a particular fun favourite throughout the year as we all shifted woodchip and sand, weeded paths, raked autumn leaves and cleared fallen sticks – not to mention the inevitable essential dose of 'larking about'.

•

For there to be a significant change in how we relate to each other in society, we need a substantial shift in emphasis from the top-down teacher-directed, knowledge-based-and-graded and time-managed approach *in the classroom*, to a more open, explorative, and uninterrupted enquiring approach *in the outdoors,* something that our environment naturally lends itself to and which seems to put everyone on an equal footing when we get out there together. Understanding others goes hand in hand with learning about oneself, a process which being together in the outdoors appears to quicken and enhance.

To learn about oneself and one's world, a relaxed and non-judgmental atmosphere is needed, where there is neither fear of failure or humiliation nor the pretence of flattery. We need to see who and what we are, based on a thorough observation of facts. Nature is probably the best hostess of this great inner work, as she doesn't compare, undermine, or label. Given the opportunity, children can sit for great lengths transfixed by the busyness of ants; they may observe their movements, perhaps mirror in some way their behaviour, marvel at their qualities, and be conscious of their vulnerability too, in relation to our potential to cause devastation to a whole colony with one small gesture. Through just observing and being, the connection with the living world grows, and alongside this appears an expanding sensitivity for oneself, for one's companions and for this marvellous planet.

•

Brockwood Park School's grounds include a grove of abundant trees and shrubs, azaleas and rhododendrons bursting with colour in spring, and majestic redwoods that can be spotted from miles around. When the flowers were at their peak of magnificence, we often took small groups of children there to observe, paint and explore the treasures of this enclosed paradise. It was a well-kept and revered place among the community at Brockwood. Consequently, we entered it as if it were a cathedral, stepping inside tentatively, having paused first at the gate deliberately so as to finish our chatter and summon quietude. One entire school year I took the oldest group of children once a week for long sit-spotting moments as part of their 'nature day' happenings – notepads and pencils with them just in case. The challenge was to find a favourite spot and return there each week to begin to notice the more detailed changes that had occurred, and thus develop a deeper connection with their little chosen patch of land, complete with its phenomena of both life and death.

Darelle found her spot, but I never discovered where it was in the whole thirty-five weeks of our visits! Ashamed now to think of it, to begin with I had suspected she had scarpered from the enclosure and taken the opportunity to move across into the neighbouring plantation of trees instead (where there were play features made by a local kindergarten). But she always appeared promptly on the soft summons of the flute and readily shared her encounters with the birds and squirrels that apparently came closer to her as the weeks went by. I knew she was basically safe, and I could sense that she was gaining and appreciating from wherever it was that she was positioning herself, so I began trusting rather than conjecturing, and left her completely alone and happily well-hidden from any human eye. That summer, she shared with her mother an account of the fox that she often saw from her spot, and how the animal, on at least one occasion, had stopped and looked at her for some time. They marvelled at how truly hidden and rich Darelle's precious time there had been.

Similarly illustrating how a communion with nature can stir the hearts of the young, five years later I received an email from Rose who had also participated in this year-long 'experiment'. Her letter arrived during the first Covid lockdown in the UK when exams had been cancelled. Instead, she was being asked to submit a creative writing piece based on a place she found beautiful, which, she explained, encouraged her to look back at her childhood and her time at Inwoods.

"Despite being significantly more distanced from nature due to the lockdown when writing this [exam piece], I felt

instantly connected with the natural world which I spent so many years held in the safe haven of. It brought back so many pure memories of the peace and safety which I found in that circle of redwoods and how I used to treasure every moment I spent there bonding, laughing and exploring. So many recollections of the hugs which you and I shared every morning as we set out on the walk to school, of the mornings spent sat in a secluded part of the Grove pouring all my thoughts out onto a little wooden clipboard! ... I feel so unbelievably privileged to have spent such a portion of my childhood in nature's care..."

•

Inwoods had the feel of a democratic school, in that it valued self-determined learning based on mutual respect, equality, and having a voice. However, it didn't employ any voting system for planning and decision-making. Rather than simply reacting to the likes and dislikes of individuals and groups, we sought to pay careful attention to both the subtle and explicit responses of children in *any* context, while as much as possible keeping discussions and questions alive. We were also not shy about trying things out and sometimes bringing in the element of freedom of choice among several stated or unstated alternatives so as to observe interests and understand better what was driving each child.

One sunny summer's week in 2015, and the last nature day of the last week of the school year, we tried out something different. Teachers offered the children the opportunity to dip in and out of their regular classrooms to explore what was on offer elsewhere and with others. They located themselves in their usual allotted spaces waiting with their helping hands (including in the outdoor playground), and the children were invited to use all rooms and areas for their innovations. On this particular day, the older group would typically be sit-spotting in the Grove. I headed over to Brockwood to collect the mini-bus, assuming that most of the children, if not all, would likely choose instead to enjoy the new sandpit in the sunshine, or pull out the Kapla and other construction favourites or projects that they were creating together across the age-bands. I was convinced that nobody would want to be sitting alone elsewhere when there was so much fun stuff going on at Inwoods itself. But I was utterly wrong. All but one child of the usual group eagerly jumped on the bus, and several of the younger children filled up the rest of the seats.

This little 'test' was the final indicator to confirm my sense of the intrinsic feeling for nature that children have and the need to have the freedom and space within it to simply be. Children need to be grounded in relationship with the earth, discovering the marvels of the world in their immediate surroundings out of their own perceptions. That means having such quiet opportunities for the quality of attention to develop and bloom, and not always being driven by previously stored thoughts and memories and the expectations of peers.

But why limit these opportunities for unhampered 'being' to the odd opportunity here and there? Fortunately, there were a few occasions when we were able to embark on a multi-day immersion in a natural setting, which raised a range of learning opportunities less likely to occur in the limited and somewhat artificial school context. With gear on our backs, we hiked to the local woods from the school gate and set up camp with bell tents and hammocks. We foraged for supper, struggled (for some) with nettle soup, ate around a fire, slept with creepy crawlies and listened to the wind, rain, and nocturnal animals in our close vicinity.

There is a danger that the comfortable environment of the modern home and school promotes a kind of self-absorbed behaviour thereby increasing expectations and demands on others for an easy and consumption-dependent individualistic life. These excursions were intended to engage the children in direct life situations with tasks that reawaken the senses, that challenge the physical body and simultaneously open the mind to something more passionate and integrated. Children are creatures of nature who are unfortunately often made to live in artificial surroundings. But exposing them to the raw elements while managing their basic needs, a very natural, almost primordial, response takes place, inspiring them to find their place harmoniously among the extended wild community. Learning that takes place in relationship with nature is not conceptual or abstract but very real and meaningful, and intimately woven with a sense of beauty and wonder for the living world.

So how did Covid lockdown affect some of these outdoor, nature-savvy children? Prompted by Rose's letter, I invited parents to share their observations. Here are a few responses:

"My nine year old spent the day beside himself with excitement discovering [in his new home], in the depths of the brambles,

a dilapidated greenhouse – he's so enthusiastic with his plans for doing it up to create a lovely environment for plants and insects, happily digging, weeding and planting, with many future plans for his project... My kids are really aware of nature's medicines – any rash or sting they will find a plant to help heal it. My son though (who usually does things at a hundred miles an hour) always stops me before I take a leaf from a plant and says, 'Mummy have you asked the plant if it's okay to take its leaf?' Of course, I haven't, and he always insists I do."

"I've noticed Tess's deep love and connection to being outside grow through sit-spots at Inwoods... It is deeply a part of her now. During the lockdown, one of the things she enjoyed putting into our days was a sit-spot in her grandmother's garden. She once came tearing into the house for a pen and a pad of paper to make a note of the location of all the nests there were in the garden and has kept track of them this year. It's a warm feeling to think of this being something that she might draw from in adulthood and also that the memory of these nest locations is now embedded in her mind."

David, eight years old, was on a long hike with his younger brother and mother. At the half-way point, David was suddenly compelled to interrupt his mother's story to his brother to ask whether it made sense for people to return to live like our ancestors and just hunt and gather the things we need. Here is his mother's written account of how this enquiry unfolded:

Mum*: "Well, I think you have a good idea, but I guess it's not quite that simple."*

David: *"Why not?"*

Mum: *"Um, well, human beings are funny creatures we are compelled to create and this means we have such complicated systems in our lives. I think it would be hard for us to return to something more basic. Would you want to give up your Lego and your comfy bed?"*

David: *"Our brains are too big. This is why we are destroying our environment. We need to think more like other animals."*

(At that moment a white van sped past the three of them and they were obliged to sink themselves into the muddy ditch of the small country road they were walking along.)

David: *"If we live more simply then that van wouldn't have to drive so fast because he wouldn't have to be making so many deliveries. And, that's another thing, Mummy, maybe it would make sense if everyone was paid the same amount of money"*

The two of them went on to speak about the concepts of Capitalism, Communism, Democracy and Dictatorship and finally David's question as to whether robots might be able to help in all of that. David's mother reflects on how her son took advantage of this time and space outdoors out of which these big ideas arose: *"The simple reflections of nature and animal life going on around him and this slow time and seemingly empty space was filled with wonder. I learnt something that day."*

Generally, children will quickly adapt and contribute to the culture that is being created, whether it is positive or negative. If the culture encourages inquiry and questioning, it can have a long-lasting positive impact on the child's choices and actions in later life. Perhaps if there was a daily connection with the natural environment from an early age, it could awaken in us an innate inclination to engage with, care for, and appreciate the non-human life forms that are essential aspects of our often-underappreciated planet. With such a foundation in childhood we are also likely to awaken our sensory faculties and develop a capacity for keen observation, thereby making learning more profound and providing a much needed broader perspective on life.

Going on a butterfly spotting trip, finding
the tick sheet of which ones we'd seen too confusing

· 11 ·

Inner Enquiry

Nurturing a living culture in which the children were free to ask questions and feel unhindered by judgements, required fostering an inclusive place in which the adults surrounding these children were also in the process of developing curious and questioning dispositions. The learning that was seen as vital in this respect was in recognising one's opinions for what they were and in not holding positions that would bring conflict that was harmful to the setting or between individuals. It meant being attentive to the contradictions arising when we might say or think one thing but act differently, feel one way but convey it otherwise, or conform thoughtlessly to the usual trends of responses rooted in pecking orders and self-centredness. In short, it meant doing the inner work on our own behaviours as much as we were encouraging the children to do.

The *inner* growth of the individual, inevitably conditioned by his or her past and by generations of trauma and societal influences, is essential to the health of the community as a whole. Also, the child's opportunities to learn within an intelligent setting naturally expand in tandem with the health of the group, which consists of both children and adults. Individuals, like droplets in water, can themselves contribute to a clear and expanding pool, each with their own fresh dose of clarity and truth, or to a murky, stagnating one when there is a pervasive dullness or too many oppositions to contend with. At Inwoods, I saw each drop as a responsible entity within its whole.

So, what did responsibility and learning about oneself in the context of the collective look like on the ground? In the same spirit of offering and inviting the children to engage in learning within a rhythm closely aligned with their needs, Inwoods scheduled various opportunities for the adults to join in, whether by personal choice or sometimes by encouragement within their means. There were group dialogues, individual parent discussions, whole-school meetings, workshops, presentations, reviews and retreats. Over the twenty-odd years, we experimented with different formats and tweaked our approaches to gain improvements here and there. However, the 'success' of these events and interactions largely depended on the moods and manners of the individuals participating. No amount of fine-tuning could promise harmony though there were a few elements that undoubtedly helped the cause; disagreement was to be expected, and, given the right space and the right context, would become a tool of reflection.

I'm remembering Induction Day in September 2017. A special day for the new parents and their children as they get to experience a 'day in the life of Inwoods' before the rest of the children return for the new school year. It is also an opportunity to have a closer exchange with these new families and set the tone for the collaborative and enquiry-based relationship that we hope to sustain. We gather at the Oak Tree, circling up to introduce ourselves and be reminded of the day's schedule and our protocols for the walk to Inwoods. We attempt to break the ice of formality and nerves with some name games and then lightness of conversation as we stroll along the route to the school grounds. At Inwoods, refreshments are waiting, and a grass space has been allocated for a nonverbal theatrical activity that the children, parents and staff participate in, humorously awakening those playful traits of ourselves. The children then explore their classrooms, while the parents and some staff run through any uncertainties related to the day-to-day functioning and their own interface with the place. We then discuss what it means to work together and be part of a school in which learning is seen to be more than just the acquisition of knowledge and skills.

So what does it mean to work together? It certainly does not arise from agreeing and accepting thoughtlessly, nor from glossing over or bottling up one's emotions and worries. Signing contracts, no matter how well worded and considered, will not leave much room for fluidity, for input, or for the unexpected. We were not looking for belief in a specific approach or ethos. With the parents, we had done our best to give a sense of the place and of its intentions via descriptions and examples, but the hard reality of life is that no amount of explanations will prepare for what's to come. Life is too rich and complex to be narrowed down into scripts and promises. And, typically, once the freshness of new relationships wears off and differences of opinion begin to emerge, half-felt images of others can start to crystallise and to take root, making exchanges more challenging and the environment around us perhaps not quite such a consistently rosy place. Humility in the face of one's human foibles and perceptions of reality, is a necessary quality in the endeavour to work together.

So as not to muddy the lines of our very practical responsibility and expertise as staff on the ground every day with the children, we told the new parents that the rhythm, routines and organisation of the activities was our role not theirs. In the same way that it wouldn't have been appropriate to drop in on the household of families and tell them how to manage their days, it wouldn't make sense for parents to tell us how to organise the day-to-day life of the school environment from their occasional look-in and multiple viewpoints.

However, we discussed with them how important it was to share every important observation, insight or experience, whether one was a parent, a staff member, or a child. Each doubt would be given the necessary attention. That all reflections were potentially valid and potentially helpful in deepening understanding, and that creative input and ideas were welcomed and needed. It was everyone's responsibility to communicate and everyone's responsibility to work through the variety of human ways (intended or not) in which that communication was transmitted and received. The day-to-day functional organisation of the school setting was in the hands of the staff, and in the home setting it was in the hands of the parents. But, the task of holistically raising and educating a child was in the hands and hearts of everyone.

Having touched on something that probably words failed to capture adequately, we headed over for lunch and reunited with the children, who by then had painted name labels, explored their playground, and established friendships with each other and their new teachers. This induction day set the tone and sincere wish for everyone to start building affectionate and open relationships.

•

For some parents, home-life became more interconnected with their child's life at Inwoods as they tarried about on the grounds from time to time, joined our walks, or volunteered in the kitchen or garden. For others, with more rigid work commitments, scheduled meetings were needed for that interface with the school. Alongside whole school meetings and gatherings, some meetings with the child's parents were just with a relevant teacher, while others took place with the presence of the whole teaching team. These were by far the most impractical of meetings because they were difficult to arrange, and those that didn't have a daily role with the child could (it was sometimes concluded) be getting on with other needed chores for the improvement of the place. However, putting the alluring goal of ever-increasing efficiency aside, these small gatherings (of all those who had some contact with the child in the week) were, in my mind, often the most constructive meetings of all.

Or maybe 'constructive' is not the right word. 'Magical' is how one colleague described them. Here is one example of what she (perhaps) meant following these mostly more than one hour-long appointments: It is the end of the day, and most parents have headed home with their child, but Wilf is playing outside with his older sister while his parents and the Inwoods team gather casually with cups of tea to a circle of seats in the straw-bale classroom. We are all a little tired; the parents, from an active day at work, and us, from our all-day engagements with the children at Inwoods. Home is probably two hours away, at least, and no doubt that thought is entering each of our heads. But something more pressing unites us at this moment, and there is a warmth between us all as we finish our chit-chat and melt into the cushions of our safe circle. We stop everything and an agreed quietness envelops the room for a few minutes.

Wilf is our pressing concern. This little five-year-old fellow, with energy for inventions, a love of poems and stories, impulsive and cute at times beyond words, is hitting out lately at other children, and none of us knows why. This gathering aimed to bring together with Wilf's parents everyone who was in his presence in some shape or form during his weeks at the school, and to share our observations as factually as possible. The challenge was to suspend any forming of individual conclusions and carefully listen to the shared array of happenings and interactions of Wilf's life that each of us chanced to witness. There was no aiming for a specific plan of action, but rather a collating of the pieces of Wilf's day until a fuller picture emerged. For example:

I heard Wilf tell Lucas that he likes playing computer games.

He was upset with his sister when she wouldn't let him into her room and was angry in the car to school.

I noticed how he was more willing to tidy his space when I gave a warning that the session was ending in five minutes.

I saw him and Max (often in conflict) collaborate on their joint sand construction during uninterrupted time outside.

He got mad at Damian for taking the glue that he was using for his paper creation.

Yesterday I facilitated a quick role-play about sharing, just before he paired up with Max, and they worked well together.

Admittedly, I expressed my annoyance with him when he refused to come in for lunch on Monday.

He doesn't like soup.

And I was cross when he pushed Luki over.

I heard Luki tell Max that he doesn't like Wilf.

There were tensions during the weekend with Gran not well, and I was short-tempered with everyone.

He is so attentive when listening to a story.

On Friday, before going to bed, he talked about wanting to learn to read.

What does he eat for breakfast?

How does he sleep?

Etc. Etc.

This collective sharing of observations and questions resulted in a richness of information about one child that would be missed if left to the task of one teacher. All of us had duties within the school day that resulted in an exchange with Wilf, whether on the 'walking bus', playtime supervision, or class activity. Everyone had something to bring to what was essentially an awareness-raising practice of the life and needs of a child, and any reactions we might have had. Parents weren't telling us how to resolve Wilf's hitting tendency and we weren't telling the parents how to parent. Simply by listening to each other, we all became more aware of who this little fellow was in the context of his different circumstances and where we might be falling short of the necessary steps to support and care for him. It always struck me how on these occasions each of us would get up from our seats and leave the room somehow knowing what to do even though an action plan had not been noted. In the coming days, we – 'magically' – experienced a happier more settled little boy whose hitting phase ended as quickly as it had arisen.

Needless to say, not all parent/teacher conferencing sessions managed to hold such a trusting space, and the practicalities of arranging them when staffing was limited meant that we had to resort to other setups. However, whatever the arrangement, the intention was to have a listening ear and be ready to drop or face any preconceived conclusions to which everyone was prone. As a result, like a good dough, these exchanges consistently kneaded themselves into an atmosphere of much care for all.

•

Whether you were a believer, a sceptic, a denier or a 'runner', it was fundamentally important not to be a *divider*.

Meaning, we were all in the same boat with this undefined task of raising and educating a child. *Belief* doesn't lead to intelligent thinking, *scepticism* most frequently leads to stagnation, *denying* risks being blind to potential truths and insights, and *running away* is very often a reaction based on fear or hurt, perhaps disguised as shyness or timidity. However, one of our tasks as co-operating educators is to recognise that we are all prone to these psychological traits as we negotiate our way through life, so let's not ever become enemies! Established schools may feel more secure in their historical reputation but what evidence is there for parents to be more confident about their long-term or whole-life outcomes? Whatever one chooses to do for one's child there are uncertainties. There was no point in falling out with each other because, essentially, we had chosen to be on this unconventional education boat together and were all equally responsible in helping to navigate the waters we would meet.

The learning community of Inwoods needed to keep a close eye on the immediate needs and well-being of each child while also putting their education in the context of society at large – not just in terms of supporting them to hone the necessary skills to earn a living later but recognising that simply fitting them into society as it is today was irresponsible and needed a more integrated outlook. As well as asking how to support my child to learn to read, as parent-educators we needed to ask how is my child going to learn to think for him or herself, to work cooperatively with others on potentially complex issues, face conflict and work through it – or more profoundly, not get rooted in conflict at all? How would we help this generation of young people to live fully yet frugally, unselfishly, compassionately in a world where competition, persuasion, and ambition are rife and normalised, and undeniably causing harm to the whole world?

One attempt to tackle these questions was to invite community members to participate – tentatively or passionately – in a forum where we put such questions on the table. It meant creating, as much as possible, a safe space to reflect on aspects of our being and actions that we have generally taken for granted and don't speak much about (at least publicly), particularly on such themes as freedom, competition, ambition, thought, time, living, dying, suffering, authority. Without ourselves realising it very much, we tend to either follow our parents' footsteps, our grandparents, our grandparents' parents, and the general trends and prominent positions around us, or rebel reactively against them all. What if we take a fresh look, neither accepting nor rejecting, and see if something new emerges when we become aware of our conditioning?

We called these sessions 'Dialogues', somewhat along the lines of what Krishnamurti spoke of when he used the term:

"So this dialogue, this conversation is not an intellectual amusement, a mere exchange of arguments – one opinion against another, or one formula against another formula, or one experience against various other experiences. Rather it is to look at the very problem itself and not merely be concerned with how to be rid of it. So we are not dealing with ideas, we are not concerned with an idea which is yours, or another's.

What we are concerned with is the fact, with what is – what actually is." (Krishnamurti, Talks and Dialogues, Saanen 1967).

Admittedly, it was somewhat daunting to turn up at a venue of discussion where there was no authority to lead it, no promise of a positive outcome, and no consistency in the atmosphere of each session. Sometimes there was an ambience of earnestness in the room resulting in an upbeat feeling for those who participated. Sometimes we could be solemn and tentative and at other times bursting with experiences to reveal, resulting in a more therapeutic vibe. Sometimes themes unfolded within a quality of listening and affection in which we seemed to be moving in the same direction together and a fresh perception would arise. I remember a new parent to the community commenting that it was like having a chat among friends but on serious stuff, talking over together though not necessarily trying to get anywhere or prove anything. I could see that he appreciated these philosophical exchanges. As far as I was concerned, all these dialogue/enquiries, chitchats and discussions among parents, friends and colleagues were a valuable contribution to the creation of an environment, like the 'play of painting', that aimed not to judge or condemn or let division dictate our relationships and influence our lives.

Whole school parent and staff meetings were another valuable forum which increased in regularity and frequency as we grew clearer and more courageous about what a partnership in education could be. These were held twice termly – near the beginning once staff had found their feet again with the children and were surer about some of their plans up for discussion with parents, and then towards the end of the term, when a time for reflection and wondering also needed a valued space. One meeting leaned more towards functionality and action, and the other towards review and enrichment, though the overall intention was to ensure that we were integrating the heart, head and hands whatever the discussion point.

Unlike our dedicated dialogue sessions, these whole school meetings were structured and facilitated with agenda items gathered and shared beforehand. They were minuted, would progress within a timeframe, *and* were strongly encouraged to attend. They usually took the format of a particular staff member or parent presenting a specific topic for all to then raise questions about, as well as breakout moments into smaller groups of parents and staff mixing and discussing something with greater depth. We experimented with all manner of ways to support inclusive input and a shared sense of responsibility for the outcomes of this important gathering. The intention was for no one to dominate or come across as more of an authority with their views, but rather to bring about a kind of collective intelligence in which something productive or insightful might arise.

Admittedly, there were times when we came with our personal agendas too and would have liked to have steered talk to a particular theme closer to our hearts or minds, given the chance; what was hot on my mind to go into in this precious relatively short opportunity together, would not necessarily be of interest to the rest of the group. While there was a monitor for the practicalities of time-managing, agenda-covering and input-inviting for these meetings, we all had to be our own facilitator of our own movements with regard to our internal drives and outward reactions to what was being said (or not said). To be orderly and inclusive without losing the spontaneity and potential depth and breadth of a passionate engagement was the task and challenge of a whole school gathering of concerned people. Sometimes it was frustrating, other times freeing to let go and die to one's inflated problem when something beyond the personal was touched on together.

•

We didn't have a 'philosophy for children' programme. We did, however, put questions to them that were directly related to a situation as it arose, or later as a theme for a dialogue-style exploration in a small group. These relevant and real situations brought energetic responses. When children complained about having a friend one day then being dropped the next, we might have asked: what is friendship? When they became territorial about their den construction, we would have reflected with them what exclusion feels like, and if appropriate, how conflicts and wars are started. When they were arguing over possessions, it was an opportunity to inquire into the implications of owning something. When a child had been called an ugly name, we also raised the questions: what is a fact? Why do we hurt others? And why do we get hurt?

Fairness was a typical theme of exploration when the all too frequent phrase "that's not fair" would be exclaimed

– sometimes as an attempt to get an adult, as the now convenient authority, to arrange 'fairness' even if it was not logical (nor particularly fair!). One such example of this was when a group of girls decided to extend their originally agreed-on break period outside. Instead of simply talking about this with their teacher, they argued vehemently that it was '*not fair*' that the group of younger boys in their view were getting a much longer break. It took a few questions to realise that fairness was not the issue at all. The issue was that they had got engrossed in a creative game and needed more time before returning to the classroom project they had initiated and were also interested to complete. The concern that the boys should have the same amount of break (either having *theirs* extended or the boys' reduced to match) dissolved once they became aware of their practical needs rather than simply demanding fairness.

Fairness is an interesting beast. I remember fastidiously counting the chocolate Smarties and dividing the colours equally among my three siblings when I was a child (note: all the colours had the same flavour, except, according to my eldest sister, the orange ones). At Inwoods, I would divide the birthday cakes and *of course* ensure everyone had the same number of pieces. Inevitably there would be a few leftovers and crumbs that some children would hang about and plead for, once most of the children had run off to play. I was reluctant to indulge these few four-limbed vultures, worried that others would claim that I was acting 'unfairly' on hearing about the extra handout. As it turned out, when I put the question curiously to a few children who were in the vicinity, they weren't terribly bothered. "Why go to the effort of making everything equal?" Yoël said, and added, "If others get to have a bit extra while I'm spending the time playing with my mates, then good for them: I get to play, they get to eat. Sometimes, I might get to eat while they get to play." – or words to that effect.

And so, by asking questions and listening to the children, our pre-formed views or strongly held positions on things were also challenged. Their views were often less anchored and sometimes more creative (and connected to a real context) rather than a carried-over idea as often occurs in the adult world. For this reason, it was better not to lecture the children about friendship, sharing, generosity and the like but allow their emotions and thoughts in the context of the incidents that they faced to speak out, so that they could find out for themselves what makes for harmonious living and what doesn't.

In this respect, I will not forget David's simple, rational comment at age seven, in which he seemed to also speak from the heart. During a sharing circle some children were expressing their woes at being excluded from the dens of others, while the excluders were expressing their woes at having too many people in their creations at any given time, and having to deal with subsequent damages. "What can we all do about this?" we asked the children. They put their problem-solving hats on and made several good suggestions, such as agreeing on the number of people at one time and setting up time-slots for people to sign up to. Then David piped up in a clear and unwavering tone and said, "Anyone can help me build my den and go there whenever they want, at any time." And added, "Just try not to break it."

Relatedly, on our 'walking bus' in the morning there would be one spot at which we would all come together in a circle for a few announcements, and to prepare ourselves before the last quiet stretch to the school gate. Amelie refused to join the circle, which was a regular occurrence with this little lass when she felt low or in a particularly defiant mood for whatever reason. Much of the time we didn't insist, but on this occasion, after some failed affectionate coaxing from the adults, Jeffrey asked the children if they had any suggestions to get her to join the circle. "We could bring the circle to Amelie", one child proposed. What an idea! And so, there we were, carefully shuffling our bodies as one circular unit until Amelie merged in at its edge, grinning from ear to ear.

We didn't ban dens, preach about kindness or punish wrongdoing. If the behaviour was awkward, inappropriate or hurtful, we attempted to address it with intelligent conversations with all those involved. That's not to say that conversations weren't sometimes difficult or without firmness and needing interventions. Aggression and bullying were not okay, but neither were punitive reactions and depriving children of the opportunity to understand themselves and be the one that instigates their change.

Change doesn't just come from attention to personal incidents. Reflections brought on from themes of study that children may be involved in or have witnessed can also lead to nuggets of wisdom. For example, when learning about the Industrial Revolution in the context of the class topic, 'The Green History of the World', we wondered together about the dichotomy of incredible inventions that brought increased comforts *as well as* forced child labour and terrible working conditions. Darelle said *'greed'* was the problem. Having inquired about his friend's personal project on WW2 and hearing that power and unresolved disputes were at source, Jonathan said, *"It's a bit like when I argue with my brother. Perhaps if everyone stopped arguing for stuff, there wouldn't be any more wars."* Even at a young age children can be wise to the destructive nature of self-interest and the connection between oneself and the world.

Vivian was enrolled for almost all her primary years at Inwoods, which included in her later years some extra tutoring for reading and writing outside of the setting, which her parents and I agreed could benefit her. Recently, I contacted her mother to find out how she was getting on at secondary school. I had watched Vivian grow to become emotionally composed and reflective in response to various situations she was encountering, but I was somewhat concerned at times that her foundational 'academic' skills were not where they could potentially have been in preparation for her next steps. Actually, I was quietly anxious that on this occasion we may have not got the balance right and I promised myself to include here whatever her mother had to say about this. The response I got was not what I had expected:

"Vivian is just wonderful, although you could say we're biassed being her parents. Without a doubt, her years at Inwoods, allowing her to grow and explore learning at her pace, have been hugely beneficial. However, I would say this caused a couple of minor challenges to begin with as she was used to expressing herself and sharing her opinion if she disagreed with things, something I don't think her teachers were used to. When this came up in discussion, I did explain

that she had been taught that every person, regardless of their status or age, had the right to express themselves, particularly if they had a different opinion, view or just disagreed. Also, Vivian knows her mind in a way many children don't, so if she says something or adds her view, it is something she has thought hard about – something the teachers have come to love about her. We firmly believe that this skill was developed during her time at Inwoods. She deploys this approach in many of her lessons by being inquisitive and prompting discussion with classmates, which has been commented on many times as she displays maturity and a willingness to take the time to listen to others and discuss their views and hers. She thinks before she speaks, but when she speaks, it is always worth listening. She makes observations about human nature beyond her years. Vivian is flying at school in all subjects, especially science and maths, and has been a team leader for drama and sports."

I believe Vivian's story illustrates that taking care of the children's mental, emotional and social health needs to take priority over targeted curriculum content. Children's insights arise from their conversations with each other and with adults, and within the context of life around them. For robust and energetic exchanges to occur, we need to foster a culture that does not emphasise a 'wrong' or 'right' answer when working things out together or exploring ideas. In this way, children can tap into that unrestricted and fluid space in their minds rather than be hindered by a constant wary eye on the disapproval or approval of others. With an uninhibited enquiring response to life, knowledge and skills can find their proper place.

To help break down these barriers to thinking, we experimented with more organised enquiry sessions with the children by valuing the process of questioning more than the arrival of any conclusion. Here's how one format operated for a time: A group of children sitting in a circle on the floor with a couple of teachers. Two piles of cards are placed in the middle: one pile has the symbol '?' to represent a question card; the other pile has 'C' to denote a comment card. A starting question is put to the group. Anyone with a further question or comment to add, rather than holding an arm up waiting to speak or jumping in and interrupting, takes the relevant card from the pile and places it in front of them. The facilitator keeps an eye on where the cards are landing and ensures people's questions and comments are raised in good time. This approach also had the benefit of slowing down the enquiry and involving all the participants. It supported those who tended to speak easily to listen more and those who often said little to speak. As a consequence, everybody seemed to have more patience and confidence in this process of thinking together.

An example of one theme explored during such enquiry sessions concerned 'perceptions'. Extracted from the book 'Understanding Me, Understanding You' by Manoj Krishna, the following question was put to the group: Two people are crossing a road, one sees a snake and reacts, the other sees a rope and doesn't react, why? This got everyone thinking. Are our perceptions influenced by our senses? What might be missed if certain sensory faculties are not used? Who were the people crossing the road? Jenny suggested that perhaps the person who saw the rope as a snake had worked in a zoo or jungle and had experience with snakes, and the other person was a builder and had experience with ropes. This led to comments about how experiences and memory may also influence our perceptions and how we can perceive situations differently from each other, potentially causing misunderstandings and conflicts.

Another format for enquiring with the children (particularly for the younger groups) was in assisting the awareness of theirs and others' emotional states. A person leading this session would gather a selection of small trinkets and put them in a 'treasure box'. Each child would choose one trinket and place it in turn somewhere on the circular rug which everyone sat around. To initiate the sharing, each child was invited to share what she or he was feeling in that moment as they placed or moved their little object. The process often developed from statements related to hunger and tiredness, grumpy or sad feelings, excitement or wanting something; ruminating on special memories or plans, incidents that upset them, worry about an upcoming event, or interest to form a connection with someone – illustrated by moving nearer to the object of someone that they didn't usually play with. This moving of objects gave something tactile and visual for children who needed a focus and structure for sustaining a quality of listening as their emotional vocabulary was being broadened.

Death was one theme that spontaneously arose out of the children's sharing in this 'treasure box' exercise. David's father was dying from Motor Neurone Disease (MND). His family moved to the area so that he and his brother could attend Inwoods. David's father wanted a nurturing place for his son and a supportive community for his wife, who was soon to be a widow. David knew his father was unwell as he experienced him progressing from an active and fully involved caring parent to a more distant person confined to a wheelchair and a breathing machine, but he was less conscious of his impending death. David's make-up was such that he rarely shared or showed his feelings. During one 'treasure box' session, the children spoke about animals, relatives and people they had known who had died. This prompted David to refer to his Dad's illness but not yet about him dying, and as the conversation unfolded with children remembering people they loved and acknowledging death, Hugo said, "I feel so calm and relaxed, I can remember sitting on my Mummy's lap, nursing." When David's father finally passed away, the opportunity and forum was ripe for him and the rest of the children to speak openly about mourning and grief. David explained eloquently to the group about MND and the fact that some diseases cause a slow death. Children reflected on what they needed or didn't want from others when they were sad about something, which evoked David to share what he felt was important for him during those sensitive days of his loss.

Emotions are too often suppressed, especially when they are frowned upon or misinterpreted, and thus children are hindered from the beneficial work of recognising their emotional states and learning about themselves in the process. When one is sensitive to the subtle sensations of anger, sadness, fear and desire as they arise in one's mind and body, one can better explore the interconnected ecosystem of emotions and thoughts before they breed devastating outward expressions that could harm oneself and others. Thoughts often trigger feelings, and feelings on their own can be an essential indicator of a situation that needs attention. One may *think* oneself inadequate when unable to concentrate, or be *feeling* and noticing the sensations in the body (tiredness, thirst, aches etc.) that are making concentration difficult. By giving both thoughts and 'felts' a quality of attention, a little window opens into the world of both our assumptions and bodily needs.

Teachers are not psychologists, and even if they were, finding out for oneself what is going on in one's mind and body is more beneficial than being dependent on someone else to tell you. For this reason, we would aim to respect those emotional moments and accompanying thoughts in the children for the potential wisdom hidden there when one holds open the space for attention to arise before any kind of labelling or interpretation.

When Rosie came to my side crying, I first reassured her that it was okay to cry. She said she was frightened. After a little while, I asked her if she felt any sensations in her body; she pointed to a couple of places and described what she felt there. It seemed there was more than just fear. I asked if she would like to share when those sensations started. Then she described the argument she had had with her friend, her reactive act of scribbling on her friend's drawing, and the thought that her friend would be so upset that she would retaliate by physically hurting her in some way and never be friends again. Thoughts were racing, and the feelings of sadness, shame and fear were intense, revealing how critical that friendship was to her. After some enquiry that included both the wordless *holding* of emotions and the observation of possible assumptions with whatever words we had, Rosie was quiet. She then asked me to accompany her to see her friend. I hardly needed to say or do anything as a restoration of their friendship happened within seconds with neither child any longer emotionally charged by their altercation.

•

For a couple of years, we experimented with writing Pedagogical Documentations (PDs) as starting points for educational enquiry. This aimed to broaden our understanding of the learning situations that children were spontaneously engaged in with each other or when on a task with a teacher. As if writing a story with the main characters being the children, we attempted to capture through photos and text the learning journey that we witnessed, describing what happened, where, who, and why the particular learning was seen to be valued. This required being present and accompanying the child or children in their initiated activity or teacher-led engagement while removing ourselves enough not to interfere but to take notes. The outcome was a creative document reviewed and discussed with other teachers and eventually shared with parents.

Someone's PD was often a little window into an aspect of a child's world that the rest of us would have easily missed. There is more than meets the eye when block towers and sandpit bridges are being constructed, or when children are collaborating in earnest on their ideas or are absorbed in a solo investigation, or when they are determined to reach a physical achievement or complete an artistic creation. The content of each PD would highlight different themes, thus also providing a window into the particular interests, values and possible assumptions of the adult that has been witness to these worlds and dared to describe them from their angle of understanding.

'How did the rainbows get inside?' This is the title of Darshana's PD in July 2017, captured on a sunny, cloudless day in the Big Barn with a group of children who are discovering what happens to light as it reflects off a CD surface. (Photos omitted):

> A commotion: a rainbow on the ceiling! *"Where's it coming from?"* Someone sticks their head out the window, others follow: *"How did the rainbow come down from the sky?" "There's no rainbows out there." "Yeah, it's not rainbow weather."*
>
> But the rainbow partly disappears. *"Hey, what did you do? It was like a shadow... "It's the cd! Stand back!"* After an uncomfortable, tense moment, someone reaches out, *"Wait wait, look look!"* As he holds the cd, his whole body shows intense focus: the plans in action, the assessing, the successes and new ideas as he makes rainbows on the ceiling, wall, faces. He isn't done, there's something he's searching for while the children around him clamour. *"When can I have a turn?" "I'm after him." "I'm after her." "I'm after her." "Put it over here, no, over there."*
>
> The rainbow has touched most of the room; he's found its edges. He reaches to pass the cd on, then discovers that two children have found more cd's. After exploring, one child carefully places his cd down and asks

me to take his picture with the rainbow. *"Look, it's on his face!" "What?" "The colour, the rainbow." "How?" "I put the cd down." "Let me see..." "Is it on me?"*

People wait, letting each other stand in the reflection, knowing I'm taking photos. Directing each other minutely: chins and angles, describing the rainbows. The room goes hushed, reverent. Bodies strain to the light, held. *"Do you feel it?" "I feel it."*

Then it's like a party: *"Come, see! It gets on you."* Children who are often wary of each other stand in the light together, laughing. Someone notices another child eating lunch. They run: *"Did you see it when I was like (gestures)?" "And then she went like (mimes)?"*

Calling out to others: *"There was a rainbow inside!"*

Darshana concludes: *The children have explored this reflection and let it lead them to discover new things. As I watched it unfold in front of me, it was life-affirming to see the threads of magic and science interwoven with personalities and relationships.*

Whether our PDs featured an emotional process, captured conversations, described ideas or investigations, all views were worth sharing. PDs, our meetings with a child's parent, our moments to enquire with the children alone or together, helped to shift our perspectives, nudged us out of our conjectures, and kept alive a spirit of asking those crucial questions related to one's notions about learning and relationships.

There was also the benefit of setting time aside for the teachers away from the school confines, to reflect together with more leisure on the roles and responsibilities in this fundamental task of being an educator. The never-ending busyness of school duties, the rich and vibrant life of the children, and the inevitable worries and questions of the parents kept us daily on our toes as we responded to the immediate needs of life at work and then, no doubt, at home. Under these circumstances, familiar, no doubt, to many teachers across the world, there was little room for the necessary time to step back and see where we might be becoming mechanical, lazy, superficial, repetitive, or rooted in ideas that hinder deeper perceptions. In the last seven years, residential retreats for staff became an important element to the ethos of enquiry that was essential to Inwoods.

These few retreat days were an opportunity to laugh and chat together, spontaneously unveil one's life story as well as aspects of our personalities that were perhaps less visible within the school's enclosure. What emerged between us was a closer connection as we went for walks in the countryside, shared in the cooking and cleaning of our lodgings, spoke earnestly about our difficulties or our challenges, moaned, mooned, imagined, and sometimes indulged in the 'what if' rather than the 'what is' of our endeavours. Our retreats took us to the Lake District, Cornwall, Devon, France, and even India. We got lost in the windy fells, exhilarated by cliff and coastal walks, and became enamoured of the crafts, birds, snakes and spiritual bustle of Asia. It felt good to put our working relationships in the context of the wider world, and to discover how different and yet similar we all were: fragile in the face of the unknown, confident with respect to a revisited experience, timid here, assertive there, sometimes competitive, jealous and all manner of traits that can get in the way of relating with affection or love. And when the ego was quiet, we also noticed how our various skill-sets, quirks, experiences, and pearls of wisdom, had the space for settling into a sort of collective wholeness.

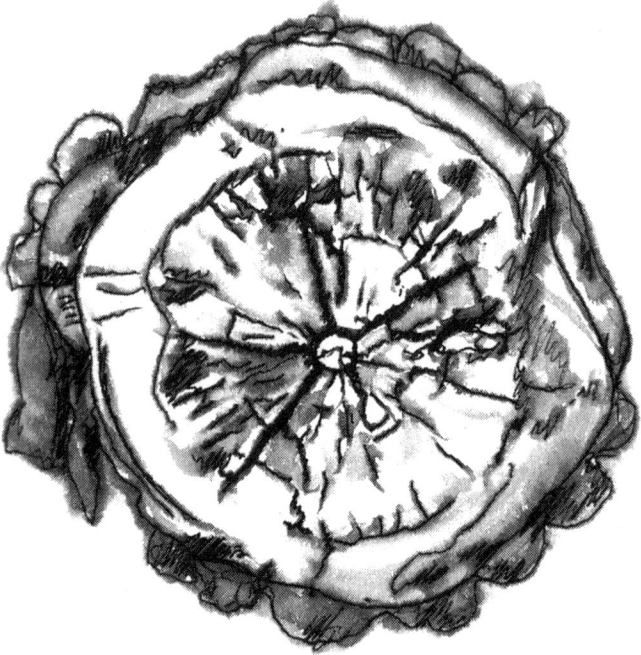

*Using stumps as seats around the fire or jumping
between them in the back field as part of a course*

· 12 ·

Broadening the Scope of a School

What if a school were a vibrant hub for change? Change that starts with the inner blossoming of oneself, inspiring further shifts to happen within the community and impacting action locally and beyond. What if our endeavours to develop ourselves within an educational setting were deeply connected to a compassionate movement towards change in society, such that ambition for individualistic gains were replaced by a feeling of responsibility for the evolution of a saner world?

School as we generally know it focuses mainly on individuals gaining knowledge, skills, and 'drive' in order, as many parents must be hoping, to find a secure niche within the accepted culture of their upbringing. Most schools, intentionally or not, will aim for the child to fit into the general trends and behaviour by which the majority of organisations function, therefore making such aspects as competition, hierarchy in relationships, and coercive strategies the prepared environment for the jockeying for jobs s/he are likely to hold in the future. Unless the adults working or co-operating in our learning settings are regularly questioning the status quo of behavioural manipulation and profit-based thinking, they will continue to blindly mould young minds to reinforce the trends that promote division, sorrow and environmental degradation.

The school has the potential to break down individualistic thinking and to put each unique human being in the context of his or her immediate surroundings: their relationship with others, with objects, with animals, plants, the soil, the walls and corners of their lived-in environment. The children need to feel connected to what is living and what is serving them, to the stories of people and the stories of stuff, so that deeper respect and sensitivity for one another and our planet's finite resources can emerge.

Developing a sense of place and responsibility for this physical venue (called a school) was a consistent focus throughout the growth of Inwoods. Whether you were part of the pioneering cohort of parents, staff and children when there were classrooms to build and renovate, or joining years later into by then well-established facilities, there was always something to clean, paint, plant, look after or create on the grounds and in the structures of this shared space. There was always some aspect of the physical setting of the place that needed maintaining or improving in some minor or major way.

Work parties were a regular event. When cupboards and shelves needed sorting, leaves required raking, dirty windows were calling for a good wipe, and outdoor equipment for a thorough tidy-up, children and teachers would get into groups and set to work with a healthy dose of team effort and energy. Some weekend hours were also scheduled for the parents throughout the year to paint walls, uproot weeds, and deep-clean the classrooms and kitchen. Major adjustments also took place from time to time: a whole shed was lifted by might and muscle and moved a few feet to give some extra gardening space; the walls of the strawbale classroom were built by a novice group of curious eco-build learners; a balance play-feature was designed and created by eager parents; an earth-oven constructed by an eclectic mix of folk from in and outside the school. Such working party days included refreshments and much chatting as hands and feet were toiling, minds and hearts were converging on important issues, and children were playing among this benevolent ambience generated and modelled by their parents and teachers.

Rather than preaching about climate change and the global plastic crisis to young children, we focused on bringing awareness to the immediate ramifications of our relationship with material things, and our responsibility to the space in which we all worked and played. There were boxes full of packaging for creative constructions, wastepaper baskets for recycling, a used paper drawer for aeroplane and origami designs, compost tubs for the garden, and plenty of corners where excess educational resources were stored waiting for potential use, rather than thoughtlessly thrown away.

Needless to say, it was a relentless task to raise awareness in different ways as to how we use, abuse, and tend the many, many objects that we were privileged to acquire at school and home. When pencils were carelessly dropped and broken, paper only partially used and then discarded, badminton or tennis rackets left lying in the mud, punctured and abandoned balls uncovered in the winter among the brambles, and bits and bobs seen floating in the well, here was an opportunity, not to rant and punish, but to consider together the journey and life of these much-used items. What energy, resources and sacrifices would have been made for us to have the benefit of them? How could we look after them better? Why would we look after them? Whose responsibility was it? Here was a learning opportunity not to be missed.

Born into a Western environment full of replicated objects that seem to come and go at the click of a button, it's no wonder that children are not naturally acquiring a sense of preciousness for every item. To encourage less recklessness and more carefulness without stifling the youthful explorative spirit is an ongoing challenge, though a wholly necessary one. It needs individual attention as well as a collective effort.

One day I brought all the mud-coated play objects: bats, balls, sheets for dens, sandpit equipment and other bits and bobs that had been left lying around, into the centre of our morning circle. Inwoods' soil was clay in the summer and sloppy mud in the winter. It was an abundant source of creative earth sculptures one season and wicked sludge creations and shenanigans the next. Endless fun, until the mud got onto the walls, doors and parents' car-seats, and prematurely buried useful equipment until it was forgotten or destroyed.

That day we needed to witness, collectively, the

repercussions of 'fun' taking priority over responsibility. I asked the children what they noticed, pulling up one dreary looking item at a time – something that was a joy to hold and play with yesterday but a repulsive nonentity today. Those objects spoke volumes. Few words were needed by me as even the questions were initiated by the children: Oops; yuck; oh dear; that's a shame; what shall we do?; I have an idea; what about this… that… Eventually an array of solutions were offered from all ages of the circle as to how to play, then put away and take care of these well-crafted objects whose components were once upon a time a 'living' thing. Information about the global crisis for powerless young children risks creating fear and despair, but brainstorming solutions as to how better to care for the elements (human and non-human) of one's immediate visible surroundings is, by contrast, an empowering affair.

Yes, it was a relentless task year after year, but when a child spontaneously picked up a hidden fork in the grass, returned a book left outside that was about to be rained on, turned off lights, or cupped with utmost care a stranded insect to release it outside, one stopped complaining. Children learnt to look after their belongings and to encourage each other to respect the surrounding wildlife: I can still picture Ollie, releasing a baby slow-worm into a safer location, saying, "let's give it some privacy" and then removing himself from the spot, waving for the others to follow.

Coordinating 'Care Jobs' and 'Kitchen Rota' with children was another unrelenting mission for the sometimes-frazzled educator. In the worst-case situations, we had to coax and chase children who wanted to 'find the fun and evade the mundane'. Calm conversations were needed to arrive at consent, and then the learning to do a job well could begin; otherwise, it was just a battle. But once the children were included in discussing possible formats for these needed chores – with songs and harmless banter agreed on – the motivation increased, followed by independence and then initiative. "We don't need your help today, Mary-Ann", Aura told me one day. "Us Redwoods (the eldest group of children) can take care of it and help the younger ones." And so I disappeared to the office for an urgent task while the mixed-age team of youngsters rinsed dishes, loaded the dishwasher, washed pots, wiped tables, swept and put away food. Perhaps the standards weren't quite mine, but it was a job completed with an initiative to be appreciated and worth every minute of those past careful conversations.

•

Looking after the precious part (the child) that has an impact on the whole, requires seeing the significance of this connection. Educators need a deep sense of responsibility for the planet to foster the necessary qualities in a child to support positive change. With this outlook, the organisation's identity becomes less important; it is simply a venue to gather, explore, enquire, and learn together. Thinking is no longer in terms of my earnings, my status, my security. Management is no longer in terms of creating a profitable institution, a marketable enterprise or an efficient system. Children are not seen as commodities. What matters is relationships and the qualities of sensitivity and care that can be nurtured within the context of an inclusive place of learning for everyone. While on paper Inwoods belonged to the Trust, in its day-to-day relationships and modus operandi it was a mini-ecosystem of multiple interconnected organisms; people with tasks, contributions and ideas who came and went and helped the environment to thrive (or not) and organically grow over time.

When it wasn't thriving, it was because we were caught in trivialities. Why? Most probably because the emphasis had swung too much to the individual, and problem-solving had become limited to fixing rather than enquiring, with issues heavily revolving around personal concerns. It didn't matter if communication was between colleagues, between adults and children, between parents, parents and staff, or regarding managerial tensions or irritations: when the issues became too self-centred, we lost sight of the whole. The reactive discomforts of having one's image ruffled, one's actions questioned, or one's hurts exposed, pulled us away from the vital work of nourishing the child's environment with the necessary ingredients for both individual development and wider change.

When no amount of thinking and talking was going to remedy the personal issues between people, something else was also needed. Something that is hard to put into words but is there when there is a quality of listening between the lines of one's conversations, or when eyes meet, arms embrace, or hands touch. It is there when we are both sit-spotting quietly with our heads to the sky, watching the birds of prey. It is there when we walk side by side, feet firmly on the ground, drawing from the earth a different kind of energy for resolution or understanding.

For that something else – whatever it was – to do its magic and dissipate any built-up tensions coming from our tangled interpersonal concerns, we needed other forums for connecting. We needed opportunities where words and thoughts could be replaced by smiles and laughter, nourishing food, music, fireside warmth, bouquets, games, performances, singing and dancing. Inwoods regularly hosted seasonal events that brought the community together both in leisure and in cooperation to prepare for them. Autumn was celebrated with hot chocolate, earth-oven pizzas, apple cakes, lantern parades, and a story around the fire-pit while roasting the children's harvested chestnuts. Spring was marked by painted eggs, baskets, hunts, presentations and games. There were bright flower-woven crowns, impressive spreads of potluck food, theatre and folk-dancing in the summer, and home-crafted gifts and winter celebratory feasts for the December closing of the year.

As we know, music, food, merriment and celebration are traditions common as much to modern cultures as to our many ancestors across the globe. And on these occasions, there was no alcohol or other substances needed for any festive enhancement. We simply brought 'ourselves', with our crafts and talents, to make something beautiful together and honour our little school, our privileged natural setting, the seasons and life itself – a life that can be joyful, light and simple when we connect with each other beyond the fixing and problem-solving mindset, and away from our personal ambitions. On these occasions nobody plugged into their digital devices. Perhaps, if anything significant is to arise out of these informal gatherings, particularly for this new generation entering the increasingly online world of work and virtual social living, it is going to be the ability to experience that joy of relationship when it is grounded in the physical presence of a familiar space, in nature, cared for and rejoiced by everyone. Perhaps, if this is nourished sufficiently when young, the digital stuff of our adult lives will find its proper place among instinctive initiatives for more tangible and varied engagements with one another.

•

Whistles, bells, alarms and shouty voices are standard tools used to alert groups of youngsters into forced speedy attention or action. In certain situations, these rather military-like strategies work to grab everyone's focus in the fastest way possible for the benefit of a specific outcome that a particular person or structure has in mind. Indeed, how else can hoards of people in an environment full of commotion be made aware of what they are required to do next? There may be no other solution for such circumstances. However, perhaps we need to remove, where we can, those conditions which train the mind to become dependent on directives from others, and which thereby encourage the abandonment of responsibility and reduce awareness of one's behaviour in the context of our shared surroundings.

At Inwoods, we experimented with doing away with 'commanding voices' in favour of nurturing a more attentive disposition and responsibility to group transitions and activities. Somewhat enamoured with an approach taken with adults at an education conference in Germany that I attended, I wondered if the same could be implemented with children. It took several chats and practices to get it working. Picture the scene: children exuberantly running and chatting along the edge of the parkland to the large gate facing the lane, all arriving in dribs and drabs, playful and engrossed in their banter. The next task is to exit the gate quietly and together, and, where cars are passing, to cross safely to the track on the other side. There is a lot of commotion. An adult raises an arm and waits. No words are uttered. A few children notice the raised arm gesture and raise one of theirs too, becoming quiet as they do so; this has a domino effect on other children who follow suit. Eventually, everyone is standing quietly and ready for the needed instruction and transition.

There were several things I noticed about this mostly word-free and collective approach to eliciting order: children were grateful for the extra time to finish their sentences; those that had become reliant or expectant on their name being called out before responding, generally became more aware and receptive to the changes in their surroundings; children who were already waiting would help the process along with little nudges and gestures to their unaware friends, thus decentralising the responsibility; adults had to bite their tongues and renounce the itch to be solely in command. Over time, the signal of arms being raised by each person was no longer needed as everyone became more aware of the increasing quiet that enveloped them. Of course, it wasn't always a fool-proof method, but with ongoing persistence and patience it became a welcome improvement to the usual mismatch of individual chaotic ways resorted to when needing to achieve order (often following a period of noisy commotion). And so, some circle times and larger gatherings had this less intrusive and less aggressive, more gentle and respectful way of bringing everyone's attention to a collective cause.

How else do we support an intelligent response in the child to their everyday interactions? How can we raise young minds not to depend on structures and roles that they learn to ride and hide behind for their assumed importance and security? If the school is not an 'institution' but is in fact the collective effect of each one of us and of our relationships and actions, what light does that cast on its role? What are our responses to a child's insecurities and courageous or hesitant experimentations? Children carefully watch our movements, our reactions, our words and our predispositions. They pick up when we are anxious or scheming and latch on to certainty and assertiveness, whether valid or not. Young children are highly impressionable, so we have to ask the question, do we actually want to impress on them *our* stances and projections, or is there a way of nurturing a mind independent of our own, one which is able to recognise any manipulative movements of the self and go beyond them? The first step is to observe how our own adult minds are functioning.

Jason told his reluctant son that if he didn't learn to read, he wouldn't earn enough to have a nice car like his dad. Katy told her daughter that Ben was horrible to act like that with her and should be punished. Matthew told his son that he would sort out the issue when he moaned about his teacher. Hidden behind these responses to the children's resistances and grumbles is the conditioning that we need pleasurable rewards in order to learn, that wrongdoing needs retaliation, and an authoritative approach is required to sort out our problems. And so children learn that desire, criticism and power (amongst others) are the levers for manoeuvring through life. This is the society (i.e. all of us), infused with conflict and contradictions, that we have created and sustained.

What would a different response look like in the face of the children's understandable protests and tribulations? How can we guide the child to think and feel through their predicaments and develop an independent way forward and a deeper understanding of themselves? I believe it begins with a genuine sense of sustained curiosity in the situation that the child has brought to our attention. It means holding back the thoughts and assumptions that might be habitually on our lips. It requires opening our ears and asking questions that stimulate our listening faculty. In return, this provokes the child to return to their natural state of feeling and noticing, and begin to say more and recognise that there is more than meets the eye in their everyday encounters with fellow human beings. Ears, eyes and lips are working on listening, seeing and bringing to the surface the very factual aspects of children's troubles rather than sentiments and demands. How did that happen? What did you notice? How did it feel? What do you mean by that? Describe a little more? Did something happen before? How did she feel? What did he think? What do you need now? Is there a conversation waiting to happen? True parental curiosity will formulate the right questions at the right moment. But more important than the questions is the atmosphere created by genuinely trusting in the child's ability to go beyond their self-centred motives and come (with or without words) to a more integrated and compassionate understanding of themselves and others.

This approach not only deepens and widens one's perceptions of the world, both for oneself and for the individual child, but also nurtures a sensitivity in all those involved in this fact-finding and non-judgmental exploration. There is usually more to uncover when we look more deeply together. Complexity is there, but simplicity too.

I remember how Georgina, arriving at Inwoods age eight, responded to an invitation to a creative writing initiative by declaring that she didn't like writing and promptly placed herself under the table in her free state of solemn protest. What struck me first was the sweeping statement, "I don't like writing", when in fact, I had witnessed her happily writing lists of ingredients for a recipe book, creating a fact sheet for her animal project, and completing a grammar exercise without any resistance at all. So, once her protesting had done its course, we had a chat about all the aspects of writing that she did enjoy and that it was explicitly 'creative writing' that she didn't seem to get along with. Once this was uncovered, it was easier to patiently feel our way together, as facilitators-and-learner of writing practice, into a gradual gaining of confidence and joy by putting pen to paper. Some weeks after this episode, I remember sitting on the bench outside Georgina's classroom and her opening the door and telling me, with a big proud smile, that she was on chapter five of her creative writing story.

The compartmenting of subjects in schools, compounds the problem of sweeping statements such as, 'I hate Maths', 'I don't like Writing', or 'History is boring', that we often hear children exclaiming. However, while it may be of value to have a more integrated programme of study, this will not solve the cultural trend of using absolutes and generalisations to describe ourselves and others in numerous situations and then hang our truths on them in response to the children. Words, arising out of thoughts, are limited, and sweeping statements and absolute phrases are mostly a shallow interpretation and often a reactive one. Thoughts simply based on memories, ideas and conclusions, are also limited in their capacity to deeply grasp the reality of something or go further in understanding our problems. And contrary to a cautious relationship to thought, education has become a hothouse for promoting methods of discourse aimed at combative arguments or 'clever' debates. Thought, and its formulation in words, is a fabulous tool but a pretty problematic one when we blindly allow it to condition our children and value it above everything else.

So, what if the role of the school, with its responsibility to the world, were also to pay attention to this incredible human phenomenon: thought. What if we were to offer within the education setting, opportunities to observe in oneself and others the movement of thought as it strives to create something, to understand something, to falsely or correctly interpret situations, when it may damage relationships or solidify views and conclusions to the point of dividing us from each other? To pay attention to thought, like paying attention to anything, there first needs to be an interest in it, some space, quietness, curiosity to observe – and no notion that there is a 'bad' thought or a 'good' thought, for that would already be thought imposing and interfering with the watching.

•

A school can be a place where the 'educators' are also learning from the children, thus breaking down the divisive hierarchical relationship which so frequently establishes itself between the youngsters and the elders: the ones who know and the ones who don't. Often this learning is subtle and not explicitly put in words (and has little to do with 'knowledge').

Lia was a sensitive child, tuned in to the emotions and states of others, and with a notable capacity to empathise when there were friendship fallouts that she desperately wanted to remedy. Lia was part of my little project group finding out about the beginnings of life on earth. Each session was kicked off by telling the story of one of the eras of the evolution of life, with some magnificent photographs to illustrate and interspersed with relevant science experiments. It had already taken several months for Lia to shed her anxious eagerness to please her teachers and become more comfortable with being herself.

However, one morning during this project session that I was leading, I experienced how closely connected she was to my state of mind and how this impacted her. The children eagerly sat down to hear the next chapter of the captivating 'Story of Life on Earth', maintaining their focus and interest until it neared snack time. At that point, my impatience to proceed and finish the section that would naturally lead to a proposed activity following their break took precedence. Suddenly my plan overshadowed the children's needs. Ignoring their squirms and disengaged expressions, I stubbornly tried to project an attitude of calm, using a few words while awaiting their attention.

Internally, though, I was becoming increasingly irritated and disconnected from everyone, a fact Lia picked up on. She displayed frustration toward the other children, insisting on quiet, only to become upset with herself for adding to the commotion. It was as if Lia had become a manifestation of my internal emotional state, and in that mirrored moment, I saw the inauthenticity within myself. That's when I decisively ended the session.

On a related note, Shaun didn't hold back in letting me know how I had destroyed his first completed creative writing achievement, of which he was very proud. Despite several years of treating children's work with respect, one day the 'teachy' part of me took over (partly induced by a looming inspection visit). Using a coloured pencil (not red) I underlined incorrectly spelled words on Shaun's personal piece of hard work. How did he react? He protested furiously with words, tears, and actions, leading to a lengthy apologetic (on my side) conversation beneath the classroom table. He had invested several hours across multiple sessions into his creation, and I marred it with my authoritative marks in minutes. Fortunately, in our family-like setting, our relationship was such that he could express himself freely, and I could wholeheartedly acknowledge my blunder.

The situation was different for my niece, however. In a recent conversation with my sister about one of her artistic daughter's school experiences, she told me how much effort and care her daughter would put into the presentation of her class work to make it look beautiful, only to find it defaced each time with marks and comments (positive or negative). "How can the teachers not be aware that they are ruining my work?" her daughter would exclaim. "Her situation was interesting." My sister explained. "Because the teacher thought they were doing a 'good thing'. She received a 'presentation point' for good presentation! Job done! But it was scrawled across her work. Really it revealed the teacher giving such a mechanical response and ultimately completely undermining it. Students are always looking for thoughtfulness in their teacher. No respect without that."

This isn't to suggest that there is no place for mark-making with a learning purpose, but rather that this warrants a conversation with the youngsters beforehand, along with employing imaginative and respectful ways to draw attention to perceived errors. Better still, rather than merely 'correcting', one could delve into the thought processes that went into the whole work, thus revealing so much more for both the student and the educator.

I've come to think that an authentic expression of oneself, despite the momentary emotional outpouring that it might provoke, is *less* harmful to our relationship with children than the pretence of goodness, serenity, 'knowing' or being 'in control'. Without burdening and blaming the children with overly emotional states, I see a need for an honest acknowledgement of one's less-than-perfect challenges in our interactions, rather than a kind of toxic 'positivity' removed from reality and giving a false representation of life.

When we peel back the layers of ourselves – the person trying too hard to be this, that or the other – and show the colourful palette of what we *actually* are, more trusting relationships can build. Similarly, if the educator coaxes or cajoles a child to participate, to perform, and thus to believe that their endeavours are either marvellous or terrible, that child will sense the game at play and lose trust in the educator. The seed of suspicion begins to root at a surprisingly early age, I believe. It causes a child to have less access to the wealth of learning opportunities, both for knowledge and *self*-knowledge, as they turn away from those that could be significant assets to their upbringing. Devoid of trust, no one is in a place to learn from the other, whether adult or child.

Honesty and humility are essential ingredients to the health of a sane world. So let's begin there. Let's make this a fundamental aspect of both the school and the home. When I looked back at the email correspondence over several years, I was reminded of the attempts and struggles to communicate with sincerity while listening to sometimes complex messages (whether accurate or not). It was an inner work not to fall into the trap of defensiveness, and to let go without a shadow of resentment.

It's an exceptional moment when two sincerely concerned people, both trying to understand something but rather caught in the net of words, becoming heated, tense, and unrelenting, suddenly, and simultaneously, perceive the futility of this trajectory of conversation and drop it all. No residue. On one such occasion, Vince and I went instantaneously quiet. Then he let go of his cooking utensils, I let go of my papers, and we simply embraced. No more words needed.

•

It takes two to tango, as they say; two or more to dance this mysterious art of relationship, full of twists and turns, ups and downs, and inclusive of many diverse and interesting beings. Throughout Inwoods' years, there were a few young ones needing assigned helpers to support learning and integration into our already diverse crowd of life's dancers.

Phaedra had Angelman Syndrome, barely able to walk, couldn't talk, smiled a lot and laughed easily, particularly when others were laughing too or being rather entertaining in her presence. She also received much pleasure from tactile sensations and would often be seen playing with the pebbles on the pathway and reaching out her arm to touch the children near her. I remember four-year-old Yoël having his curly locks stroked during circle-time, not in the least perturbed by her intimate gesture. It was hoped that Phaedra would eventually learn to communicate using sign language, so it became a school-wide effort to teach Makaton signs to many of the children alongside her personal tuition.

Hilda had a characteristic wide smile that became a cheeky grin at times, with an occasional additional mischievous twinkle in her eye which admittedly put us a little on edge, wondering what she had just got up to. Hilda was physically active like all the children, and drawn to our craft supplies, particularly the addictively fascinating electric sharpener, which we eventually had to remove due to new pencils quickly ending up as pointy stubs. Until then, it was a collective effort to keep an eye on this rascal of a lass and the dwindling pencil box. In fact, children became little experts at stepping into her creative world of explorations when they were sometimes going amok, learning to be fearless to her barks of disapproval while getting to know the gentle jolly soul beneath.

Anne was a sensitive and inquisitive young lady, very affectionate and with many questions, including quite profound ones at times. Rather than reading, writing and mathematics, her interest was in people and places, resulting in a remarkable capacity to remember the stories of others and situations she had joyfully been a part of.

Navin was on one end of the autistic spectrum, coming in just one day a week from London to be surrounded by our nurturing setting in nature. And Ana, hearing impaired and with cochlear implants, joined her elder sister at Inwoods because it was simply the most natural and rational thing to do for the whole family. In another school-wide effort, we learnt to use the wireless hearing-assistive technologies needed for group sessions, passing the microphone from one speaker (adult or child) to the next so that Ana could hear us. We were all learning about the limits of her hearing faculty and worked enthusiastically to support her integration.

These individuals had one thing in common: they all had

an adult helper accompany them throughout the majority of their Inwoods' days to support them either physically, academically, with behaviour, or with speech improvement. The task was to provide the right kind of attention for the specific need while ensuring full integration into the life and lives of the Inwoods' setting. It was interesting to witness newly enrolled older children start by interacting awkwardly or not at all, then gradually develop creative ways of communicating that were not based on verbal negotiations and the usual social banter. Something in these children and the way their 'carers' cared, elicited the tender aspects of even the roughest of rascals.

When one values the fostering of trusting relationships and learning from each other (whether an adult or a child), seeks to understand beyond the word and thought, and sees the danger of institutionalised thinking, then the school naturally becomes a catalyst for community building and change. Community that is not based on contractual obligations but a sense of earnestness to dialogue on all manner of concerns and grow in affection for one another whatever the background and temperament. Community that is not limited to the school walls and boundary fence but also extends to family, friends, neighbours and beyond, because its members have seen the urgency to reach out, take in, protect and nurture their connection with their surroundings – be it human, animal, plant, landscape or object.

Out of our human innate inclination to learn and grow, and within a welcoming space given for this to happen, Inwoods was able to be more than just a school in the traditional sense. For those who embraced this potential, individual gains were less at the forefront. What matters is the greater work of our humanity in which relationships are not fragmented or broken through habitual thought, but built and sustained out of affection. Enquiry is not just about information but arises out of wanting to learn about oneself in the mirror of one's relationships. And status is dropped when we are no longer identifying ourselves with the organisation or with one's role. Anyone at Inwoods could instigate a dialogue group in the school setting or in their own home. Enrichment workshops, parenting groups, listening partnerships, walks, and invites to local environmental events and talks were welcomed initiatives as contributions to the critical work towards inner and outer change that could also be the responsibility of the 'school'.

One ongoing and challenging aspect of my role was to describe Inwoods' intentions to prospective parents and visitors as accurately as possible. One morning, just a couple of hours before an Open Day, I tried a different approach and jotted down a list of what Inwoods was *not*. And so, I end this chapter with this list of why we were not a school in the more conventional sense:

1. We don't push the children on a trajectory of learning that complies with government standards; And therefore...

2. We don't follow the National Curriculum yearly targets; And because of this...

3. We don't penalise parents for taking time off for

their child to travel, engage in educational trips, enjoy holiday extensions, or simply for rest and family time;

4. We don't value knowledge and academic skills over emotional, social, physical and artistic learning and creative thinking;

   And therefore…

5. We don't coax the children into pursuing academic targets that they are not ready for using rewards, comparing or shaming techniques;

6. We don't feel valuable learning is restricted only to a school environment and to children;

   And so…

7. We don't keep parents at arm's length so that they can't have any input in their child's educational journey and possibility to learn alongside teachers;

8. We don't believe in moulding a child's brain to fit into a sick society that values consumerism and personal gain at the expense of others and the environment;

   Which is why…

9. We don't create an ambitious atmosphere that blinds us from seeing and acting meaningfully with regard to others and nature.

Excitement around the nest that appeared in the Oak Barn's straw which could be seen through the window into the wall

· 13 ·

Families

All the families that joined Inwoods did so – as parent Jeffrey put it – with a certain element of 'bravery'. Most enrolled following several visits, a certain amount of correspondence, chats on the phone, and one or more prospective days for their child, which often included mum or dad, or both, hanging about on the grounds for part of the day to observe the interactions with their child and assess the atmosphere. It seemed essential that there were no surprises, and for everyone to be seen in all their guises in which they might be 'walking the talk' or falling short on certain aspects of the intentions. Rather than enticing new families by a perfectly crafted day, it was necessary for them to witness the reality of our small alternative school initiatives, and to actually *feel* our heartfelt intention for us to join forces with anyone wishing to be a partner in the mighty task of educating a child within the context of a fast-changing and troubled world. What was most important to identify was whether there was a mutual interest to work together with care, giving the best of ourselves, for ourselves, each other and the children.

Needless to say, no amount of visits and chats were going to portray the full reality of life at Inwoods or predict the whole truth of where we were stumbling or thriving. A lot depended on financial and managerial constraints humming away in the background, varying from year to year and often beyond our control, and, of course, on the day-to-day evolution of the child, who was unpredictable and certainly not mouldable in our eyes. You had to see this and live it to understand it. Families came and went, but I would like, by way of example, to dedicate this chapter to three families, distinct from one another, yet among those who sustained the Inwoods experience to the critical end. Families who gave their hearts and minds to the project within the limitations of their circumstances, at the same time *themselves* changing and developing, challenging us, contributing to the melting-pot their doubts and wisdom in the shape of questions, proposals, their child's behaviour, and through their relationship to the whole community and educational venture.

Let me begin with Sarah and Lindsey, with their son Xander. Sarah and Lindsey were owners and employees of a small family printing business that survived recession-induced years through their sheer hard work and dedication. They were barely in a financial position to afford the alternative education that they wished for their son. Education for Sarah had always been important; having been raised to believe that academic success was the best measure of a person, and primarily defining herself that way, she loved learning and sailed smoothly from school to PhD. However, over the years she grew to realise that there was much more to education than *"book learning"* and wrote in her own words that *"such a blinkered outlook risks missing so much of the wider picture of life, and endangers emotional and personal growth. An open and enquiring mind can lead you to all sorts of amazing places and offer so many opportunities outside the confines of other people's expectations of success."*

When Xander arrived in Sarah and Lindsey's life, the purpose of education became a serious concern and took on a wholly new meaning in the context of their busy work-life circumstances. The burning question for them was how to nurture a young mind and body in such a way that they would develop to their full potential, while encouraging a love of learning that is not dependent on exterior motives. Initially they chose to home-educate, but this soon became unsustainable as the demands of their business increased; consequently, they enrolled Xander in the local infant school where they managed to negotiate part-time attendance for the first two terms. However, according to Sarah, it became apparent that Xander's *"individuality, personality and enthusiasm for learning were gradually draining away under the everyday routine where conforming to [the school's] social norms and achieving arbitrary academic targets was more important than nurturing the small person that was [their] son."* As Xander began to lose his spark, and his parents' initial fears became a reality, they realised that this was not going to work and that they had to find another way.

Xander attended Inwoods for three days a week during the first eighteen months. In that time, he developed from a slightly unsure young five-year-old into an emotionally confident and happy six-year-old, with a wide circle of friends across the ages and genders who have remained close to him to this day, now a teenager. Xander could relate respectfully with children and adults alike, and seek out learning as a source of pleasure rather than duty. Each holiday he asked to bring home some of his favourite classwork to do with his parents, thus becoming a key bridge-builder between home and school.

I remember Xander being a little awkward in his movements, seemingly not as agile as some of his peers, which was noticeable when he ran somewhat gawkily across the playground, and clunkily skipped-rope with innocent determination. However, according to his parents, his *"physical confidence . . . increased exponentially with the ever-present opportunities he had for climbing, running and swinging in the beautiful grounds of the school."* When asked by his slightly disapproving grandparents, "so what do you do at your new school" he chirpily and rather wonderfully replied, "climb trees!" He was unabashedly challenged by some outdoor physical invitations and sporting offerings while generally flowing with the more scholarly stuff. That was the child he was then. However, he embraced both essential fields of learning with equal interest, advancing at his pace and holding a distinct notion of excellence.

Damian and Ollie, brothers, were two very different children. Ollie, the younger of the two, was probably the most physically agile child I have ever met. The Inwoods grounds, despite containing a substantial number of trees, swings, logs, outdoor play-features and sporting equipment, could not challenge Ollie enough, and we had to keep a careful eye out for him in case he scrambled up a tree too high or sneakily put himself on the shed roof. He had a petite build, long hair, and slim muscular limbs great for swinging between branches. Sit-spotting sometimes became tree-hanging: I have a wonderful snapshot of Ollie upside down in a tree, legs hooked over a branch, arms dangling limply, eyes closed.

On one occasion, I discovered Ollie curled up inside a car tyre with a friend's hand just about to launch him off a grassy slope. "It's perfectly safe", they exclaimed in front of my dropped jaw, "Look!" and off he rolled before I had time to risk-assess this somewhat hazardous looking feat. Ollie could also engage with other, less physical activities, but *that* was often on *his* terms and required a high degree of explorative input to sustain interest. Communication was more corporeal than verbal, so we knew instantly when he was gung-ho or not about something, as in the latter case he would quietly take off to occupy himself elsewhere according to his liking. Working together with him to develop his language and receptiveness for the more nuanced interests and relationships, those which also form part of a young person's learning and life, was an ongoing objective.

Brother Damian was a boy of few words but for different reasons. His speech was unclear; he would lisp and slur his words and form incomplete sentences, making communication sometimes difficult. In his first few years, aged six, seven and eight, he bumbled along enthusiastically; exploring, playing, 'trying things out' like many of his peers, while also receiving some extra guidance from various adults when learning in a group appeared limited. As Damian grew older, we observed an ongoing enjoyment for tinkering and messing about with craft items, and a particular love of woodwork. We didn't have the resources for more one-on-one adult time with him, and so found ourselves drawing on the care and skill of some of his classmates (Xander being one of them) to read with him or sit next to him as he manipulated the maths materials. These were touching moments to witness as the children embraced their teaching role with seriousness and complete acceptance of who Damian was.

Who Damian was, was also a mischievous lad who would find an infinite amount of 'fun' (his word) in creating pranks and scaring some of the younger children who were less familiar with the friendly chap he really was. In a desperate attempt to put some boundaries to his behaviour, we began to recognise that he didn't have much of a moral compass at the time, so any imposed consequences to his actions didn't result in an improved sense of responsibility and actually risked dampening his self-worth. His headaches, sensitivities to ambient noise and challenges with communicating made focusing, following instructions and learning with others demanding. But he had friends. He had adults who respected him and who provided high-quality attention whenever they could. He had a varied and flourishing natural setting, and had parents who were fully committed to working with the staff, the school, and the community to the absolute best of their ability.

Ollie and Damian's parents, Lilly and Nathan, joined Inwoods in 2013. Nathan was a graphic design and visual communication teacher and the primary breadwinner for the family, while Lilly took on the bulk of the interface with the school (like many of the mums), getting immediately stuck into every aspect that would help her connect with the place and people, and simultaneously learn about parenting two lively lads. Neither Nathan nor Lilly were looking for a specific approach to education to suit particular ideals. They were looking instead for community, and for a slow start to life in which learning for them was as important as learning for their children. They wanted a whole family experience.

Lilly described being particularly smitten by the aesthetic environment of nature and natural objects: wooden tables and chairs, cloths, rugs, cork, boxes and baskets, rather than the bright and overly gregarious furnishings that many schools adhere to. "The children at Inwoods had the space and time to unfold in their own way as opposed to being enticed or coerced into learning." she told me. She was also drawn to the warmth of a family feeling, where the kitchen was an extension of the classroom, and one could lend a hand there while the children were engaged in activities elsewhere, or indeed were themselves joining in with the chopping of vegetables.

Lilly and Nathan's personal experience of education was in the context of a relatively poor rural location. Nathan, diagnosed as dyslexic, was bullied by teachers, which eventually led to him taking frequent bike rides rather than turning up for classes. Lilly loved art but hardly got to do any of that at school. Both of them felt that, ultimately, their teachers didn't (or couldn't) care much for them as young maturing human beings.

Jeffrey, Isabel and their son Juan have altogether a different story to tell. When they first heard about Inwoods, they were living and working in Spain as language teachers, and attended an education fair there in which Brockwood Park was represented. It wasn't until they visited Brockwood in the summer of 2015 that they discovered Inwoods also existed under the umbrella of the Trust. Following their trip to the UK, I received an email from Isabel asking if there were any places left at our August week of workshops for children. Apparently, it took only the first fifteen minutes of attendance at the opening circle on the first day for Jeffrey and Isabel to be clear that Juan's education would continue at Inwoods. Mother and son arrived in the UK (temporarily accommodated by former Inwoods parents) in time for the 2015 September start of the term. Jeffrey had to stay behind due to work commitments that could not be quickly ended.

Juan was eight years old at that time and a quiet, shy boy with a meek presence and consistent curiosity for life. Originally from Bolivia, he was adopted by Jeffrey and Isabel at the age of fourteen months, having experienced twelve months in an orphanage. Though Jeffrey was English, Juan was more fluent in Spanish. His limited knowledge of English coupled with his father's absence during his first year at Inwoods was a challenge for Juan, and there were some months in which it was a little 'touch-and-go' in terms of completing the first school year.

One occasion in which two girls called Juan a 'weirdo' alerted us to the possibility that friendships weren't being easily formed due to some of the children's discomfort with his different looks and quiet Bolivian mountain temperament. We had work to do to understand some of the children's reactions to someone seemingly different from themselves, though equally in need of respect and companionship. How were we going to help the children see the significance of bonding beyond language, looks and character traits? Such seeds of prejudice can easily germinate within an inattentive institutionalised setting. Fortunately, those few offensive shoots withered and died, though we also learnt that socialising wasn't so crucial to Juan at that time. He appreciated the company and respect of others but valued his personal space to engage in artistic pursuits and connect with the natural surroundings, rather than 'working at' forming strong bonds with a group of lively (sometimes boisterous) youngsters.

Educationally, Isabel and Jeffrey were keen that Juan have a gentle-paced approach to learning in line with *his* needs and confidence, no one else's. It's important to note that Jeffrey not only moved to the UK to join his family for Juan's second year, he also became a full-time teacher and thus a vital member of the school. He was one of the few privileged parents to witness the interactions and development of their child within the milieu of a 'school' environment on a *daily* basis, so he was well placed to observe the facts of his son's learning in the light of his ideals.

After a year of enrolment, some teachers wondered if some tutoring would benefit Juan. I think many parents would have jumped at the offer, but Isabel and Jeffrey responded in writing with the following sense of clarity and trust in their child. *"We are both well aware that academically speaking, Juan is 'behind' for his chronological age. We, however, remain confident that his full potential (whatever that is) is within himself and will unfold when he is ready. We, as his adoptive parents, are willing to respect his rhythm fully. Our objective is for him to grow as a healthy tree. All that the tree needs from the outside world is the right conditions (water, sun, shade), the authentic information the seed has within it does the rest. We find Inwoods offers, without a doubt, those right conditions for a school environment, the rest is our responsibility, the school can't do it all, of course.". . . "If you ask us"*, they went on to say, *"he has all the right conditions to blossom: Love, respect and confidence in him."*

"The school can't do it all" was the statement that struck me most. With an attitude of shared responsibility and a realistic sense of what was possible and necessary, we were able to enter into a working relationship that was much more than simply trust or 'you do your part, and we will do ours'. Like all the children, Juan was unique on the one hand but susceptible to the same emotions and subject to the same basic needs as virtually everyone else.

With one eye on the uniqueness of the many individuals within our inclusive setting and the other on the factors common to us all, we navigated our unpredictable days together as staff, parents and children. There were wild and messy times to embrace without fear or shame; but also tame, chilled days for *recuperation and reflection,* and moments when all sense of seeking, striving and struggling had ended because the relationship with another had grown into something genuinely affectionate. At the end of the day, isn't it this that matters most?

For these three families, an affectionate connection was

essential to them above anything else, and of course, they weren't the only folk who felt that way. Other important aspects that these families were concerned with that transpired, I believe, out of this affectionate base, was the functional health of the setting. It goes without saying that a certain appropriate level of infrastructure is needed to attend to any school environment's various requirements and educational elements. Equipment, resources, people and an unlimited amount of energy and generosity were required at Inwoods to find the extra money, expertise and willing pairs of hands to hold the place intact.

Lilly initiated several work parties, organised a couple of sponsored sporting events and regularly volunteered at our summer workshop fundraiser. Isabel coordinated two of these workshops, pouring all her heart and available spare time to bring in a substantial sum for our bursary 'pot' and potentially recruiting other families in the process, having enrolled her child at Inwoods via this route. Sarah organised a yearly fundraising auction of goods and services. She kept a close eye on the level of involvement needed from parents, encouraging them to chip in and lend a hand, and also to make an effort to communicate anxieties and uncertainties rather than stewing over them in the form of car-park gossip.

Sarah felt that some of the Inwoods staff were like swans gracefully moving about on the surface but 'paddling' a hundred miles an hour beneath. She saw some of us with many hats: teaching, administrating, communicating, planning and coordinating, relationship building, developing the grounds and curriculum, facilitating meetings, recruiting, fundraising, policy and report writing and so on and so forth. Indeed, it was unceasing from year to year, with some aspects taking a disproportionate amount of time away from what was essential in my eyes, though not vital enough in the eyes of societal standards and expectations. Contributing to the overall Trust's monetary pot was also a necessary prerequisite for many of its governors. They were understandably reassured to hear numbers were increasing but due in part to the lack of regular contact with the school community, didn't seem to recognise either the challenges or the tremendous potential which accompanied that.

Sarah's experienced position as a long-standing parent and her concern for the future of the place for those yet to come, prompted her and Lindsey to write a well-thought-out, intelligent proposal for an inclusive steering-group or committee that would provide Inwoods with a more sustainable long-term structure for decision-making, visioning, and staff succession. I imagined this group evolving into a kind of life support system that would empower those in direct relationship with the children and families to focus on the quality of learning and enquiry without the headache of administrative issues.

School parents are often regarded as a drain on the establishment, but when institutionalised thinking is dropped and the right kind of involvement is invited, they are capable of having an even greater understanding of the health of the place and its requirements than those with a rather remote managerial status. Many of us on-site supported Sarah and Lindsey's proposal, but it neither met the satisfaction of the other department directors at the time nor reached the governing body in its detail and so was 'shelved' in the hope that there would be a more suitable time for its presentation.

Of course, Sarah, Lilly and Isabel weren't the only parents who were very active on the ground and in their contributions to the wellbeing of this small community school. The movement to accept people from all walks of life brought richness to the place that also helped us to act and think beyond our ideals, conclusions, prejudices and comfortable positions. There was more to life than designing the 'perfect' school. In the same open-minded spirit of embracing family life that is uncertain, changing, evolving, with babies that we didn't pick-and-choose to fit one's circumstances and desires, the school was one large family of characters with fluctuating needs, requiring above all an alert and attentive energy for its members to feel integrated and cared for.

That was then. Now, these people are able to reflect on their days at Inwoods as they navigate the even larger domain of our 'one planet family'. Xander, for example, chose not to attend secondary school due to its competitive vibe, large numbers of children, and the inevitable pressures to participate in the social media world. Instead, he is steering his learning at his own pace with the help of local learning centres and online courses. He is working with enthusiasm and independence towards the nationally accredited certifications in the hope that this could potentially open doors towards advanced fields of study at some point. His interests are in English, maths, geography, physics, chemistry and history, with a particular leaning towards a social ethics and philosophy group.

Damian settled for a while into a home-education set up with a personal tutor, an arrangement that provided uninterrupted focus on some specific skills resulting in wanted progress, though it was an unrelenting task to acquire the necessary funding from the Local Authority. Ollie joined his brother at home after first attempting a secondary school setting but found the uniform too restrictive, the relationships uninspiring, and the rules and regulations pointless, having been reprimanded for taking his jumper off without permission when he was too hot. Ollie's free-spiritedness was not going to succumb to the confines of walls, chairs and seemingly irrelevant information, so one day he walked home, and that was the end of that. The family have sold their house and are currently travelling the south of England to look for more suitable schools that they could partner with and would attract their children.

As Isabel and Jeffrey predicted, there was no need for extra learning support at Inwoods; I am told Juan's potential is *"unfolding"* as they expected it would. Photography, drawing, sculpture, piano and harp are his current artistic and musical favourites, with maths and English being approached with confidence and hard work. He has recently completed an exam in Spanish to test the ground for potential other national certification routes. Like the other families in this chapter, they chose not to insist on a conventional secondary education with its nationally predetermined subjects, outcomes and required pace. Instead, Juan continues to discover his interests, try things out and then commit to a programme within the respectful environment of his home and the smaller venues of his immediate locality.

Close friendships and a social scene are still not something Juan is asking for, neither are his parents artificially trying to create them for him despite our western societal values for a thought-based articulate and wordy connectivity with others. "It needs to come from inside.", Isabel has assuredly told me, "It's not something to be forced." However, the stunning wordless mountains of the British landscape are what Juan is growing increasingly fond of, having recently hiked to the top of Scafell Pike in the Lake District, with Snowdonia in Wales next on his list.

I asked these families to reflect on their time at Inwoods and to share anything of themselves or the place which they wished they or the school had done differently, as well as any specific takeaways from the whole experience. Lilly wished she had been less anxious and had relaxed into a more practical engagement with the school regarding some of Damian's specific needs at the time. She lamented the overwhelming sense of taking a different path, hopeful of a better outcome, though fearful that it wouldn't work, something which was compounded by their financial struggles back then. Sarah felt that perhaps a more consistent approach with curriculum content would have benefited the children, and Isabel wondered if Inwoods had been a little larger, perhaps there would have been more children attuned to the quiet temperament of their son.

Lilly and Sarah spoke of the deeply affectionate and honest relationships, despite differences in personalities, that their children had established and grown to expect of others. Sarah was thankful the school didn't use comparing strategies to entice the children into action, as she is now able to witness how non-judgmental Xander is towards others and himself. All three sets of parents highly valued the family involvement of enquiry, learning and participation, and the emphasis and respect for nature. All three told me (two without my asking) that they would certainly do the whole thing all over again.

So, what is the point of this tale of three families? Indeed, it is not to prove that Inwoods was 'successful' in any way, though, admittedly, I have chosen three families with an evident fondness for the place who have benefited in a number of ways. No doubt there will be those with similar sentiments and others with more critical accounts, especially if priorities differed. Perhaps, what these three families most illustrate is *an interest to be actively involved in their child's education.* Not to twist and turn that education to suit their expectations, and so demand outcomes in the way that parents are often feared for, but to be part of an environment that is valuing something other than results and standards. A school that remains a 'people's endeavour', encapsulating a depth of engagement with life itself rather than pushing for a predictable if hypothetical future prospect, is less likely to become a life*less* institution.

In my view, school needs to be an extension of the family, a way of life for all those involved, rather than a promise from someone above for a predetermined outcome for those who can pay. It needs to be the kind of world we would all love to be a part of, though not in any way an idealistic place either. A world in which everyone matters regardless of size, age, colour, gender, nationality, faculties, traits or class, and which values relationships and learning, with all its messiness and travail, above everything else. A place free of deliberate judgments, manipulation and individual gain at the expense of others. A place where each person can be safely attentive to the potential self-deceptions of one's mental states, and therefore grow into adulthood with greater awareness and humility in the face of *all* of life, both familiar and the unknown.

*The different festivals, specifically the Autumn Festival
and its traditional apple pressing, crumble making
and bowl washing around the well*

· 14 ·

Working Together

What motivates us to work diligently and tirelessly together through the 'thick and thin' of our endeavours? What inspires us to eagerly turn up at our workplaces, engage wholeheartedly with our colleagues and creatively think through problems together? What is it that sustains a sense of purpose and meaning and generates the continuous renewal of energy needed for the day-to-day tasks and for relating with others?

There are many inspiring places for learning. At first glance their facilities appear attractive, their written words seem spot-on, and, with a closer look after a few days' visit, one is touched by the dedication and skill of the team. However, it is only when one fully *lives* the intricate life of an organisation that one can get an insight into one of the most fundamental aspects of all: how everyone there is working together. While resources, money, efficient structures and skills are all important factors for any education mission, it is, I believe, the quality of relationships that is the real jewel in the crown; relationships that work through healthy disagreements and opinions with consideration for everyone's well-being, both in the context of the child's precious life and with a sense of responsibility for the whole of humankind. This is one of the greatest challenges and crucial to enabling a far reaching transformation of hearts and minds.

For all those working on the ground at Inwoods, there was consistently a strong sense of responsibility for the children in their care. How could there not be? The children were, after all, being entrusted to us. Parents reminded us of this daily as they passed their child's hand into ours or asked a question loaded with uncertainty and worry about all manner of life issues that their children were facing or expected to face.

In the presence of a baby or young child, we are generally moved by their sensitivity and vulnerability, and their utter dependence on us for survival and for having the best first encounters with life. We instinctively approach them with softer voices, gentler hands, wider smiles and greater prudence. But as they start to grow a little more robust and independent, more questioning and assertive, our interactions tend to change accordingly and take on a more reactive and imposing manner, increasing in frequency and force as numbers of these vibrant youngsters gather in our homes and classrooms. Some hearty firmness may be necessary, but not at the expense of squashing their intelligent questioning and natural responses to their unchosen circumstances.

When our intention shifts from a tender nurturing of a human being into the world through caring observation and interaction, to taking charge of someone's life on the basis of ideas rather than actual circumstances, we begin to condition them to further the discordant aspects of our planet. Nurturing a young baby mostly consists of feeding, holding, ensuring some positive stimulus and activity for learning, and promoting enough sleep for renewal. There is much love present, and an intrinsic desire to protect against any traumatic experiences. This we need to maintain throughout a child's life, not just for the very young, guiding them with nonaggressive words and actions. However, supporting each other to do this at Inwoods meant fostering an environment in which each adult was also valued, cared for, not micromanaged but given the space to learn and make mistakes amidst trusted colleagues, thus setting the tone for a working and enquiring relationship in which no one would be functioning out of fear.

It is June 2018 and the end of another active Inwoods day for the children. Not the end of the day for the teachers, however. It is 4.15 pm, fifteen minutes past our due start-time for our Thursday 'Teacher Meeting', and with the term and year close to concluding, there is a lot on the agenda. Not everyone is here yet. Yolande is arranging transport for her sons' trip home over 20 miles away. Frances is clearing up the last remnants of her afternoon craft activity. Lynette finishes her impromptu though valuable conversation with a parent, while Darshana rounds up a more formally arranged one in the converted shed next door. Sam, Teacher Apprentice, is ready and waiting, chatting with Shayla, whose session he attended. I have my laptop open, checking the list of topic items collated from everyone during the previous days. Some children can be heard still playing on the grounds around and among their chatting parents while the kettle boils and Jeffrey takes orders for cups of tea – as always, taking care of us all with this simple, familiar, and universal gesture of kindness. Ah, that cup of tea…, after a busy day and fuelling the promise of another necessary and important meeting up ahead.

Typically, I am a tad nervous and also heartened to be in this cosy space, sitting together with my colleagues on a round rug, fortuitously appropriate for this gathering of respected equals. I look around to take in the atmosphere and mood, tuning in and out of the chit-chat, awaiting the last person to enter the room, close the door behind themselves and settle on their cushion. I want this meeting to go well. I know how tired everyone must be but how important it is for us to unite in this way after several days of going about our duties, with sporadic exchanges now needing a more thorough consideration from all ears. We are all seed-sowers in this little garden called Inwoods, all carrying our various, different and similar tools, and now here we are together this afternoon about to discourse on ways to make the 'soil' even richer. Somehow, whether individually or collectively, we all need to be working towards a sense that this education is also relevant for the whole of humanity. Darshana suggests a few minutes of quiet to bring us to the present moment.

We share notes on our observations of the recent prospective children and what brought their parents to our unusual setting. We discuss the new groups for the new term, our end of year performance, and the dates for our enrichment / 'training' days. Topics for our upcoming review of the year are brainstormed, with a long list emerging from the practical to the philosophical, from collective needs to personal wishes, from minor adjustments to ideas for major changes. Questions, statements and viewpoints enthusiastically enliven our intimate space, along with the inevitable sprinkling of patience and irritation, frankness and tact, humour, laughter and egocentric human behaviour, that we are all prone to in varying degrees depending on what triggers those little or big insecurities that we might be carrying around with us. We are an eclectic group of affectionate characters, finding safety together to express ourselves, while being mindful of the precarious zone where subservience or dominance can break a relationship.

One particular thread running through this Thursday staff meeting was 'Team Care', mentioned more than once and in different ways. While no one person can be in charge of the well-being of a team ('team' being the operative word), I felt particularly moved to support any initiatives and suggestions that could bring a greater depth of collective empathy and consideration of the individual challenges each of us might be facing. This could be in relation to teaching, pastoral matters concerning the children, workloads and tasks, or more personal issues that one might be burdened with and therefore unable to give of one's best. With everyone being different, and at different points of comfort on the privacy scale, it required all of us to tread sensitively, respectfully, impartially, sometimes apologetically, and most of all with a tenderness that each was capable of expressing in their unique way. And so, in this spirit, we developed both structured and spontaneous ways of interacting and listening, and each within a variety of venues and settings. A walk in the woods, a circle in the shade of a tree, a tearoom and my own garden close by became a frequent or occasional place in which the uninhibited parts of ourselves spontaneously surfaced, vitalising our Inwoods deliberations with a combination of leisure and earnestness.

Very little was decided on without the inclusion of most minds and hearts. Open communication, shared input, reflective practice, restorative chats, and suggestions for ways through which everyone could have a voice, choice, and the opportunity to be creative and participative in important decisions were welcome. Inevitably this made meetings long and contact time outside the school day and its duties a regular necessity. The aim was to foster as much as possible an inclusive spirit and an unambiguous dynamic, free of the ranks and statuses of more traditional decision-making structures.

The collaborative, enquiring culture of team care, team learning, team effort and input can help ease the burdens and stresses for any individual, and facilitate more minds and hearts to come to the forefront. Consequently, a kind of self-renewal arises for both the individual and the whole setting. To work organically with change we need self-organising processes rather than imposed ones: observation and awareness rather than imitation and instruction; taking one's professional development into one's own hands rather than depending on the direction and management of someone else.

The sporadic part-time staffing that was unavoidable in the earlier years of Inwoods made consistent collaboration a challenge; however, the fuller-time staffing situation that we were finally able to achieve brought a different and interesting issue of its own. When people saw an organised and well-attended little school with seemingly firm roots and a decent reputation, there was the expectation that a *method* had been devised for an alternative practice, and specific training for this would also be part of the package. However, the flame of learning-and-growing with the children always needs to be kept *alive,* and any overly teacher-trained technique risks interfering with that. Our staff meetings, retreats and informative workshops were, therefore, forums to nudge and prod each other into developing into those adventurous, proactive individuals that the children needed to be surrounded by. They were opportunities to support each other to embrace a challenge or an unfamiliar learner/ teacher setup without worrying about 'messing up'. They were occasions to laugh together at our little quirks, acknowledge our skill-sets and unique ways, and grow in confidence and clarity with every new experience and insight. Needless to say, this came with a host of challenges and frustrations depending on one's relationship with that invitation to professional freedom. As Jeffrey puts it:

> *"Inwoods – as lived by me – bravely carried and lived out the intention of being a place of collaborative, community-inspired learning and teaching, living and giving. I use the word 'bravely' because it was in itself an ambitious intention to put into practice. And it was all the braver, given the wider context of the world/ the area… in which most people spent most of their time in far more hierarchical settings where they were told, and would tell others, what to do, and*

how. 'Brave' and 'ambitious' then in the sense that Inwoods –
and anyone anywhere with similar beliefs – would always be
swimming against the tides of mainstream society, in which
many are swimming along, blissfully or painfully unaware
that the tides exist. So Inwoods was an invitation to learn
about the tides and how to swim in healthier directions.
It didn't intend – I believe – to shun any person, belief or
approach to life – but to create a space where learning could
be accessed more genuinely. The type of learning that was of
deeper life skills and insights that would serve a person to
live more healthily and meaningfully through a lifetime. The
type of learning that's a potential lifeline."

Objects, timetables, hazards and routines can be managed but not people. People need an atmosphere of care and affection, free of fear, to non-judgmentally observe themselves and learn together. Authority is so powerful that it can convince people to kill or hurt another human being or passively allow this to happen. Authority permits us to destroy the planet's resources and intimidate and divide us from one another within our organisations, no matter how small. To raise the young to be free of these destructive effects of coercive authority, we need to raise them to be sensitive and aware of their psychological movements and intentions within a setting where the adults are doing the same. We need to provide a culture and safe atmosphere that allows us all to respectfully question the other's motives while equally exploring one's own. We need to be given the space to think things through independently, logically, compassionately, and be attentive to the tendency to comply or resist. We all need the opportunity to observe ourselves in the here-and-now, so those insights can arise, resulting in thoughtful action rather than reaction, compassion rather than corruption.

When there is authority, there is no real relationship. When there is no relationship, there cannot be any truly intelligent conversations. Without intelligent conversations, we cannot work together. And if we can't work together, how can we possibly learn, grow with affection, and contribute towards a better world?

•

Being a small place, we were blessed with the chance to function informally, starting from meaningful human contact. However, over the years, we learnt that for organisational matters, it was important to be orderly and rigorous while careful not to become institutional or dogmatic in the process. With the changeability of families, the uncertainty of finances, and the challenges inherent in developing a different approach to education that could promise no guarantees, it was crucial to create as much stability as possible with regards to the core team's potential to work diligently together and with the parents, for whatever the length of their employment. Certain structures needed to be solid and steadfast. In providing a daily, termly and yearly framework for functional purposes, inevitable changes and challenges in relationships had a better chance of being navigated and facilitated with less strain on the rest.

Duties beyond the classroom tasks needed a termly consensual reworking and adherence to. This meant whoever walked the children to Inwoods in the morning or back again at the end of the day for collection, supervised lunch or the playground, cleaned up the kitchen with the children or stayed back to do the general end-of-day tidying and lock up of the buildings, did so with an agreed expected sense of accountability and commitment. Nobody was put in those roles in an *ad hoc* way. Daily chores, weekly staff meetings, termly parent presentations and discussions, and parent/teacher appointments, were painstakingly scheduled into the timetable ahead of the return to school and after much consideration for staff availability and other extenuating circumstances. Reviews of the term and year with teachers or parents, in whatever shape or form, were also an absolute must for checking that there was substance and saneness to our endeavours and no one was mechanically following. Often, we scrutinised the running of all aspects of Inwoods with a fine-tooth comb to make sure that not a single essential element was deprived of a reconsideration.

While I was a 'key player' in setting up these needed structures and processes, everybody appeared to feel responsible and dedicated to sustaining them. Even at the end of a tiring Winter's school day when the majority of us were feeling the pull and temptations of an earlier than usual evening of homely comforts, there would be at least one person who would disagree with the rest about cancelling that afternoon's staff-meeting. And so we would ungrudgingly go ahead, restored by our colleague's more resilient mood and readiness at that moment.

There is safety and stability in gentle rhythms and routines, communicated timings and schedules, shared notes and minutes that capture our momentary insights, ongoing concerns, tasks agreed on and pending actions. If order is crafted out of a shared sense of clarity and out of observation on the ground, rather than an imposed idea or an imitation, then the rest – the unpredictable, experimental, creative, spontaneous, intuitive, and relational – is allowed more freedom of space to fuel the most important work of all: the growth of the individual in the context of the collective, and for the benefit of the evolution of the setting in its responsibility to the world.

•

It goes without saying that many of the more attractive educational outcomes that have been mentioned in these chapters first went through tricky, sticky – occasionally even thorny – processes. While inclusive of certain ideals, Inwoods was hardly an idealistic place; some experimental fumblings were part of the process in arriving at our more desirable educational outcomes. It was often a delicate dance and dialogue between changing certain structures to adapt to the important needs of an individual, and sometimes seeing together that it was not the structure that needed changing but something more fundamental in the individual, or all of us.

Probably one of the more irksome aspects of working together was how we faced – collectively or separately – 'wicked issues'. These were seemingly unresolvable issues that re-presented themselves regularly from year to year. And no matter how creative we were at trying to address them, they appeared to be too anchored in the psyche of our humanness for a simple, durable solution of sorts. With each year's intake of new parents, children and staff, there would be the same types of assumptions and disheartening comments sparked all over again by someone or other: another teacher criticised for their manner or methods; another child vilified for their behaviour; someone getting heated about *others* not chipping in as much as themselves; a complaint from a neighbour about too much use by the community of the shared lane, to name a few. I have to admit that the unrelenting 'wicked issue' of muddy wellies blocking the entrance to each classroom, as children kicked them off in their eagerness to get inside, was a rather welcome one by comparison. Quite frankly, it offered a kind of respite from the seeming complexity of the rest… thanks, kids!

Many of these issues were not fixable for the obvious reason that they were neither factual at source, nor simple, and not intending to cause harm. Their origins were deeply rooted in the assumptions and conclusions of our reactive and complex minds, where fear sits, and unresolved hurts are played out in the form of biases, jealousy, possessiveness and all manner of psychological motions. Also, it is important to add, these issues could be reinforced by our own quick reactive minds in response to those traits in others (that we are also prone to if we dare to notice). We are *all* responsible for the 'wicked issues' that we perpetuate by our actions and reactions. Over the years, I learnt that they were not fixable because, in trying to fix them, we were more likely to *affix* them instead, such was the nature of these types of problems. Through observing my own and others' stumblings, I learnt that in trying to confront the 'unsolvable' of our human psychological dynamics, we risked creating a ping-pong of lengthy disputes.

Confrontation can easily include and sustain the flavour of opposition. The last thing we wanted to be doing was wasting energy in quarrels when the educational life of our children was in our hands. What was needed was an unrelenting freshness of response, always giving the critics the benefit of the doubt. Which meant, acknowledging the possibility that hidden somewhere in any reproaches and moans was actually a gem to be sought out. And that if someone gave the other a bit of compassionate space, then together a more profound understanding would emerge which is far better than any likely and futile one-sided action. This is how I also learnt to be mindful of the 'us versus them' or 'me versus you' mentality. And this is how some problems, often trapped in short- or long-rooted rumours, would either organically dissolve or not grow to become monstrous energy blockers.

•

Perhaps, it is not *just* the school that should be at the heart of our endeavours, but rather the tenacious commitment and genuine intent to work together with others, whatever we are involved in. It is a marvellous thing when people come together despite differences of opinion and experiences, and work compassionately to unravel our individual and collective thought processes and deeply-held assumptions. Such energy and clarity are generated! And the affection and friendship free of any obligation to align oneself gives an immense sense of meaning and new potential to one's life. Out of this form of interaction and connection, even if it is short-lived, something precious to humanity has a chance to emerge.

The rich, inclusive and affectionate relationships at Inwoods with colleagues, parents and children, were undoubtedly what fuelled and sustained the ongoing hard work, joyful practice and relentless determination to create something meaningful together. From my perspective, everyone could bring something significant to the setting despite each of our relative 'shortcomings'. We were all guardians of the children's lives, curators of their learning opportunities, and wardens of the beautiful natural surroundings by which we were often inspired and uplifted. But, for the realisation of a holistic educational community, *everyone* involved in some way needs to be a custodian of the crucial and demanding task to work together with diligence and care.

*A particular moment walking down the road behind the
'back garden' and the Christmas celebrations including secret santa*

· 15 ·

The Perils of Management

Management was also a factor in the life of Inwoods Small School, but not in the way that is conventionally understood. As defined by the *Chambers Dictionary (1998)*, 'Manage' can be "*to train; to handle; to wield; to conduct; to control; to be at the head of; to deal tactfully with; to contrive*". A 'manager' is defined chiefly in relation to a firm or business with a product in mind, or one "*who organises other people's activities*". Clearly, these definitions were not in keeping with the educational vision of Inwoods at the time, with its non-coercive and inclusive approach, hardly intent on becoming a business. There is a different vibe and way of working when no man, woman, or child is *deliberately* managed. However, given the widespread human tendency towards domineering behaviour, our opinions, preferences and standpoints will need transparent and careful attention if we are to avoid an imposing way of relating.

This chapter sets out to demonstrate some of the more subtle, knotty, and frustrating issues inherent in managerial constructs such as titles, positions and appraisals. It includes an account of our attempts to address these with a non-hierarchical, shared form of functioning, as well as a note on how one area of this collaborative model was critically overlooked.

Large or small, a school is a multifaceted, pulsating hub of activity and complex relationships. And the headteacher's remit amid all that is, let's face it, a daunting task for any individual who has been made 'solely' accountable. Role descriptions for headteachers can run to several pages with responsibilities ranging from staff recruitment and retention to pupil welfare and curriculum development, site-safety, infrastructure, and all the policies, communication, and financial oversight essential to their implementation. All these responsibilities expected of the typical headteacher role suddenly and inevitably landed on my lap. I say 'landed' because when appointed to this title by the Trust I was not forewarned of the lengthy list of 'accountable' duties, nor given much advice or instruction as to their execution. Consequently, it was a somewhat naïve dive into the elaborate domain of regulatory compliance, administration and organisation, made possible due to the collaborative spirit, *and*, dare I say it, a healthy disregard for many managerial conventions and nonsensical 'politics'. 'Headteacher', therefore, was a title I used sparingly and chiefly for bureaucratic purposes.

The 'Headteacher's Office': there was no such thing at Inwoods. In fact, for the first sixteen years, there was not even an office – unless one considered the small barn-cum-walk-in-classroom-cupboard an office; not large enough to seat two people though it did have a little window and a shelf just about wide enough to put a laptop on. Some years later, we made use of a small second-hand shed (approximately 2 x 5m), discovered advertised in a shop-window and then re-constructed and rather ambitiously used also as a tutoring room, library, and general overflow space. We even managed to squeeze a double sofa into the narrow width of its floor area to give some semblance of a non-intimidating cosy 'corner' for discussions, as well as a place for a poorly child to lie down while waiting to be taken home.

Scheduling this multi-use space around office phone-calls, admin tasks and meetings, was one challenge. Tolerating cold toes and fingers in the winter season while conducting interviews was the real test of our credo. Before insulation was eventually installed, I remember on several occasions sitting with my gloves, hat and muddy wellies discussing Inwoods' intentions with a prospective parent couple, all of us indoors but wrapped up in outdoor winter gear in supposedly serious 'interview' mode, while the wind blew cold air through the gaps in the floorboards beneath our feet. The decor and my demeanour couldn't have been further from any stereotypical professional image of a 'headteacher'. So, while closing the door apologetically, I would instead seek solace in the thought that anyone choosing Inwoods after such an unconventional rough-and-ready appointment at least wouldn't be subconsciously fooled by the persuasion of the 'professional-look'. In those moments together, one had only the sincerity of heartfelt words and warmth to go by – for both parties.

Eventually, in 2014, we excitedly upgraded to the

cute, stand-alone, one-roomed little brick-house, hitherto used for Mature Student accommodation, that we had had our eye on for several years, waiting for it to become available as our dedicated office space. Despite our general unpretentiousness, I rather liked the taste of what felt like a sudden 'promotion'. And, naturally enough, I was also excited by the prospect of improved order and work conditions for our hard-working, part-time admin 'assistant'. While the converted shed had been operating as our meagre office space, I had never felt entirely comfortable increasing the needed presence of admin help *there*. Now this *warm* room, with desks, space for a printer, pinboards, and ample shelves for files and other paraphernalia, made possible a proper consideration for the practical realities related to order and coordination. 'Coordinator', I believe, was a more fitting title for my actual function, and now finally there was a fitted, functioning, shared space that would benefit all those contributing to the coordination tasks – which, of course, was everyone.

School environments are often entrenched in *top-down* structures, the 'pedestal of knowledge' and the 'accepted' power of the adult. And because of a system in which large numbers of children are grouped and shuffled from one set of tasks to another, while the accompanying teacher-adults are 'managed' so as to fit in and produce the expected results, there is little scope for evolving a child or teacher's mind that might approach life very differently. The emphasis is rarely on nurturing connections or working cooperatively towards a harmonious planet, because we get too lost in the daily details of 'winning' and 'losing' our personal battles, thus teaching our young to do the same. These environments significantly contribute to a fractured world in all the various ways by which they succeed in coercing, through manipulation, rewards and punishments, thus instilling at the same time the belief that people *must* be managed. To function differently as a school, we would do well to remove labels such as Director, Head, Superior, Manager, etc., or at least the hierarchical structures that risk arousing those arrogant postures and misleading authoritarian notions which interfere with a more shared endeavour.

With our newfound school office facility, the challenge was not to let it develop the intimidating traits typical of a 'Headteacher's Office' – a place, sadly, frequently associated with reprimands, 'lecturing', or trepidation. And so, when sensitive conversations took place there between teachers and children or their parents, we all had to be mindful not to slip into domineering ways or feel intimidated once the door was shut. I remember one parent admitting to feeling a little nervous in this relatively more 'formal' setting, despite our previous years of comfortable exchanges, hence many of us took to meeting around the picnic-table, or taking chairs out to the shade of a tree, where the ground beneath our feet seemed to provide a more neutral footing.

Thankfully, our office admin companions, during each of their respective employment years, had an eye for reassuring, homely features. A vase of flowers, a soft sofa seat, cushions, and a little table with coloured pencils and paper were therefore conscientiously included in the setting. Children's drawings were pinned among the official literature on the walls, and there was a hand-painted artistic 'office' sign on the front of its bright yellow door. But most importantly, there was an air of warmth and welcome all day long – an open door (literally and figuratively) for all community members.

Was it an efficient space? Heck, no! Much admin work actually got done when the grounds were empty and quiet at the end of the school day, or back at home, or in between the phone calls and knocks on the door, if one's focus was sharp and keen enough that day. The unfolding of something more significant took place in this shared office hub when a child needed consoling, a parent needed a listening ear, or a teacher needed to discharge tensions, share questions, or simply enjoy a chuckle. Much of the time this was a far more important use than the shuffling of papers and the tapping of keyboards.

The 'Go-To-Person': a hindrance to creating a non-divisive culture within many organisational structures is the 'go-to-person'. We already see the tendency emerging among children in how they quickly figure out who to go to when they are looking to get what they want, whether that be which parent at home, or which teacher at school. Similarly, this arises even among themselves, as they discern who the influential ones are in the playground, or who is the most lenient adult to their desires. Popularity, superiority, and feeling indispensable can all be rather desirable states for the go-to-person, dangerously clouding our responses if we are not careful.

But this stuff of the 'playground', if not attended to, will continue to play out among our adult exchanges. Seeking out a second opinion in the face of a tired, 'stroppy' parent or teacher who is unable to apply themselves in a particular moment, is probably a reasonable thing for a child to do, but learning to manipulate situations for one's own agenda, or becoming dependent on others to tell us what to do, is not something we want to be fostering in our educational places. A go-to culture is reinforced by either putting oneself in a central advisory or problem-solving position or else in seeking such a person out, not necessarily with ill intentions in mind but nevertheless causing rifts and rivalries, when all those who would benefit from being brought together are left out. It can be a blurry place to navigate when evidently certain tasks will need an experienced eye and one doesn't want to seem indifferent or unsupportive to someone else's significant concern. Assigned roles for specific skilled tasks are certainly necessary, but the hidden authority of the 'go-to-person' has become quite normalised in our workplaces, often severely preventing opportunities to work through issues together and discover common ground.

In my 'bureaucratic' role as 'headteacher', I was predictably selected as that 'go-to-person' at the beginning of my engagements with anyone. I often found myself resisting this (perhaps sometimes too much so). It was one thing to try to resolve school-wide organisational issues related to scheduling, facilities, and anything material-based, but another to step in and direct, mediate, or try to resolve other people's wants and dilemmas that I had not been privy to or had not fully observed. Not only did it seem counter to our non-hierarchical ethos to have a 'go-to-person' for this, but I honestly felt unable to elicit an intelligent response or a decision *unless* I had been immersed in the issue myself and had everyone's perspective and sense of things. A shared sense of responsibility and judiciousness is more likely to arise out of inclusive involvement rather than merely relying on someone with a particular status.

Teacher 'appraisals' are another interesting theme relevant to the 'go-to-culture'. The model policy for this, supplied by the Department of Education UK (2019), sets out the regulatory requirement for government-maintained schools. It states: *"The headteacher/CEO of the trust or other senior trust staff will be appraised by the governance board, supported by a suitably skilled and/or experienced external adviser who has been appointed by the governance board for that purpose."* The headteacher, according to this document, is required to decide who will appraise other teachers, and *"each teacher will be informed of the standards against which that teacher's performance in that appraisal period will be assessed."* It is an evaluation system, based on government standards and specific, measurable objectives with *"pay progression"* as one of the determinant outcomes. What an ordeal!

To be fair, I imagine many schools do their utmost to ensure the process is as positive and non-stressful as possible, despite its obvious inherent issues. Fortunately, as an independent school, Inwoods was not subject to this nation-wide appraisal regulation. However, if a teacher had already experienced such an environment, there was occasionally a certain expectation for a bit of 'evaluation' of one's personal 'performance' from a nominated individual.

One day I was nudged by a teacher into taking on an appraisal role and fooled myself into thinking that maybe I could do this differently – tick both boxes, so to speak:

the 'professional' one which required feedback specifically from the headteacher, with the less performance-focused approach of the Inwoods ethos. Alas, the results were an awkward nondescript bit of feedback on my part as I realised that despite my notes, there was not much substance to my comments. He, on the other hand, reviewed his work and involvement adeptly, which led to the two of us deliberating on interesting and concrete aspects of Inwoods that would have benefitted all the teachers had we done this exercise together. What started out to be quite flat and mechanical evolved into an insightful discussion once those artificial aspects of our roles had been dropped. Following this, collective termly and yearly reviews became an even stronger aspect of our 'management'.

This 'go-to-person' theme is not yet exhausted. What about the 'hirers' and 'firers' of our schools? Who decides to appoint a new member to the educational setting? Indeed, who appoints that 'who'? And at the risk of sounding ridiculous, who appoints the 'who' that appoints that 'who'? It's rather an arbitrary and skewed approach to recruitment when the process is driven by an act (or even sense) of *entitled* responsibility to this dangerously subjective but important event. The recruitment of a team-player needs the whole team's sense of the candidate's depth of interest and seriousness to work together. So, at Inwoods, after the joint interviews, prospective days and casual chats among children and parents, there was nothing more than the formalities of paperwork in the recruitment officer's hands to complete the task. It was overall a relatively straightforward and inclusive approach.

Less straightforward, however, were the dismissals. I know I may lose the reader here (if I haven't done so already), but if we genuinely want to remove fear tactics from our environments, we need to be consistent with this across all of its members, not just the children. The staff also need to feel that they can work exploratively, make mistakes, learn from others, and request support without the prospect of being fired looming over them. They need to know and *see* that conversations are part of their work experience. That, if necessary, role adjustments can be made to achieve the best outcome of their functioning. And, if a particular task needs someone else's expertise then this could be sought out, thus bringing individuals together to work and learn as partners. We are not pre-designed machines made to perform specifically designed roles set by others. Rather, we are an eclectic mix of qualities and shortages of skill sets that don't need someone else's arrogant judgement and rash 'fixing'. Of course, I speak here of an educational place, a place of learning – for everyone. Not a business venture whose mission is often precisely to create a specific and profitable product or service that outcompetes other companies' endeavours, and where the hire-to-fire 'go-to-person', is part of the cogs of its machine.

In the history of Inwoods, there was only one 'dismissal'. A momentous event. It was a long-drawn-out process that included, nonetheless, the input of most of the staff then present but needed an intervention from external players. Occasionally, this may be the only way out of a crisis. Nevertheless, on reflection, there are things I wished we had done differently. It prompted us to strengthen how we were collaborating, communicating, reviewing, and, most of all, doing our best to ensure that no one was getting hurt. In the normal course of events, staff came and went for various reasons and all of their own volition. It obviously releases a very different set of feelings to leave a place when *you* feel the time is right, when *you* feel you have given of your best, *and* feel respected for your input and qualities, *and* can see for yourself, given all the circumstances that have been looked at and mulled over *together*, that it is time to say a heartfelt goodbye to a place and its people (who are sincerely thankful for your contributions). This was the spirit in which we wanted people to come and go, neither creating over time a cosy niche for oneself nor, when the time came, heading off in wounded disgruntlement or resentment.

Of course, due to the extent and pace of the work required, or simply the timing, not all decisions could be conducted in the most inclusive way desired. Some element of trust also needed to be cultivated – trust arising out of the humbleness of one's actions and not from an expectation of one's status. Moving forward, I would be interested to experiment with more visible *consensual* processes in which rounds of sharing and agreed actions are captured more explicitly, thus ensuring that someone's relevant thoughts on a matter don't slip through the net.

However, there is no fool-proof formula that *guarantees* right decision and action. More knowledge won't mitigate against the ugly manifestations of greed for power. Methods and tools are not going to *make* us intelligent and caring. No ground-breaking solution can be bought off the shelf to fix our collapsing world. If critical thinking, responsibility and compassion are essential principles to nurture as part of transformative education and our concern for humanity, then we all need to examine the mindsets behind our roles and titles, and our tendencies to sustain the status quo by putting people in positions of power. As put by a professor friend with many years witnessing the different ways of running a school: *"Rather than working with a diversity of experiences, managerial thinking sustains a monoculture and is in turn sustained by the passivity of everyone who is compliant."*

Many organisations tend to function with a pyramidal structure consisting of layers of roles, managed by a 'chain' of authority to maintain specific structures and systems perceived necessary by one or several more remote actors at the top. Often this results in fragmented parts working in isolation, limited by lack of connection with other parts of the operation and missing a sense of perspective of the whole. This approach hinders individual growth and creativity by prioritising efficiency and performance over other factors, causing members to fear losing their positions. The outcome is an institutionalised mindset and conduct driven by the abstract imaginations and sometimes arbitrary personal wishes of certain individuals at the expense of creative collaboration. Thus neglecting not only a saner evolution of the place but also the well-being of many of its members, and a wholesome relationship to the wider environment with which it interacts.

An all-too-common subtle but perilous trait of establishments is when the seemingly good-intentioned manager with his or her developed craft of 'handling' people, doesn't see that they have become, over time, clever and aloof, and believing they know what's best for the organisation or an individual even without concrete evidence from the ground to substantiate this. It's also likely that their decision provides a side benefit to securing their own position within the structure, or is a result of fear that if not seen to be aligning oneself with influential others, then they may lose their leading role. Such roles are problematic for those that are in them and for those that have expectations of them.

'Management' may sometimes hold places together by hook or by crook, but without working closely with the people who bring life and substance to the core mission, it becomes a cause for concern on a far greater scale. What value is there in a well-established educational enterprise if the people closely involved do not have the means for continual self-renewal and inner growth? Places survive with all manner of conventional managerial pathways and strategies, but, analogous to the boiling frog effect, the people there risk becoming gradually complacent and dangerously unaware that something vital and alive is being lost.

.

Despite an evolutionary process that was as much as possible grounded in the here and now of the needs and love of the children, some of us had also been motivated by dreams and aspirations. Gradually expanding our age range and enhancing our facilities to provide sustained support for certain children and families felt like a logical progression. I envisioned that one day our land would foster a deeper nature-oriented learning environment, also to include more capacity for growing our food. We saw the scope to create an inviting space to run workshops, host enrichment days, accommodate overnight guests, and engage education students who were already knocking on our doors from further afield. Essentially, I had hoped to open our space to a wider range of interested individuals, creating a small yet vibrant hub for education-related inquiries and learning.

However, while we were careful to avoid some of the traits, tactics and pitfalls of conventional management structures, there was one important element of our functioning and unfolding that was dangerously overlooked: the 'go-*through*-person'. That was me. And this was not from my own deliberate doing but seemed preferred (I guessed) because it was the least troublesome way for the governing body and their team to handle their relationship with Inwoods within the complexity of the various broader operations of the Trust (and which, to begin with, we did not see as a critical issue). I was the only one in the Inwoods team invited to governance meetings. I was the exclusive writer of the termly reports for governor perusal and was the only one to discuss requests with them, their responses having to go via me to the rest of Inwoods and back. More crucially, seldom did they come to see things for themselves.

In short, one person was the sole spokesperson and advocate for the Small School's needs. The sole small voice for both presenting and negotiating, while also trying to build a bridge between the two schools when time (for everyone) was a limiting factor. It was only in later years that some of us began to see that the somewhat wobbly bridge was not being met with the same enthusiasm for crossing and strengthening; that the one voice with its limited wisdom was not inspiring the deliberations of the wider Trust's members; that someone was carrying an unsustainable burden. Moreover, additional 'stakeholders' (parents, staff and patrons) surely needed to be part of the wider management mix and visioning. This unusual lack of inclusive engagement and cooperation with a small school's members on the part of the governing body eventually led to abrupt decisions that were not in accord with everyone's expectations, resulting in a period of confusion and upheaval for Inwoods.

A school has the possibility to be more than a haven for a few fortunate children. By welcoming the fresh eyes and experiences of individuals from diverse walks of life we can learn from each other, unravelling solutions to deeply ingrained issues within our education systems, while an impartial and thoughtful 'management' entity acts as a catalyst for transformative developments.

Sound, transformative education empowers learners and teachers to have a broader perspective on society and a deeper understanding of themselves. Rather than becoming followers of methods and passive recipients of knowledge, students participate creatively in their educational experiences while learning how to reflect both critically and compassionately, and thus becoming important agents of change. A wider change is needed no matter how small or large one's setting and whatever the context. Firm and kind questioning of the power relations at play both within our organisations and around us is called for. By putting in place structures that value everyone to the best of their function and potential for input and insight, we can draw on the goodness that lies within us all.

Through education we can learn to do things very differently; commune with each other with depth and attention, humbly alert to the inner movements of our hearts and minds when separation is in action. More important than getting one's children and students into prestigious universities or into well-secured life-long jobs, is to awaken intelligence to such an extent that division, rife with conflict and sorrow, is no longer the stuff of life.

What if, rather than seeking and creating managerial structures in the name of outward efficiency and self-protection of an organisation, we urgently pursued a more connected and pliable way of functioning together? A different action arises from the ground and a different atmosphere pervades the structures when we are in touch with the needs, the beings and the practical circumstances of life. All the necessary nitty-gritty decisions can then emerge from a shared and close observation of what is factually there, provided there is patience, interest and we dare to care.

Sometimes found around the swings of the 'back field',
reminding me of the tyres, Easter egg hunts, and the parachute

· 16 ·

The State of Education

Life is learning, and the manner of our learning seems to be deeply connected to our relationship and responsibility to life. It is the process by which our perceptions are enriched and our insights expanded, thus unlocking the potential to hone necessary skills and attributes needed to carry out a task and intelligently put it into its broader context. It is what connects us to our actions, to each other, to nature and our surroundings, to grow in wisdom and wake up to the great mystery and meaning we are a part of.

Learning by doing and observing, listening and questioning, practising and experiencing – never concluding! – are all possible due to the faculties of the body, mind and senses when one is free to think, feel, observe and be attentive to both the inner and outer realms of one's being. Without this capacity to learn broadly and deeply, we would become dull and mechanical, or reactive and impulsive, and potentially destructive to ourselves, others, and the wider environment we all inhabit.

Life and death, joy and suffering, learning and relationships are the facts and challenges of one's existence. Intelligent education, I believe, has an urgent and vital role to play in deepening our understanding of everything contained there and within the context of our enduring, multi-faceted world crisis, in which nationalism, consumerism, division and violence are wreaking havoc on our planet and hindering our potential to be psychologically free.

Does the scope of a 'normal' education even begin to teach us to respond to the events of the global crisis, intelligently, and with compassion? Our formal education, thirteen or so years of it!, rarely touches on the two most intimate of companions, life and death. Fostering an attention to our human nature is something which most schools neglect in favour of academic accumulation. And it seems to me that, in general and global terms, our self-destructive tendency is unfortunately what is actually being cultivated in our schools, else how would we have reached this present state of our world?

Education, as it is now presented within our standardised institutions, is largely limited to only some aspects of learning. Here, it is wrapped and packaged with definitions to fit its agendas, and with methods and infrastructures to achieve its objectives of – regrettably – generally shaping the learner in some way or another, and mostly to fit in and sustain the current model of society. Many of these institution's values are largely fashioned by unconsciously imbibed ideas, ideals, ideologies, or dubious authoritarian (or simply unthought-through) agendas by people with control, while employees go along uncritically, preoccupied by their positions and personal securities to survive in a competitive world. As such, and instead of taking responsibility for their own learning, teachers and students must navigate from one fragmented and limited learning setting to another, as fashions in education change according to who politically is in power, thus being kept distanced (perhaps conveniently) from the facts and fundamental issues of our world situation that drastically needs understanding and changing.

At best, the education setting can indeed be orderly, efficient, and subservient to its hierarchical structure, able to achieve some element of quality in a particular area for those that quietly fit into it. At worst, it is inconsistent, conflictual, and even harmful to those with no other choice. Many dependent young learners come out the other end either fitting dubiously into society by blindly or deliberately contributing to those self-same structures that perpetuate harm of some form, or are lost, outcast and drifting through life as one psychological pain builds on another. There is something sacred in a child's innocent natural passion for learning about 'everything', and in their happiness at being alive. Sadly, an education geared to making the child into an obedient and efficient cog in a society that is ultimately destroying the planet, is producing too many youngsters, as we see today, who are miserable, stranded, and who have lost their natural drive and sharpness for learning.

How many of us are honestly content with our education? Were we given the skills and knowledge to contribute positively to the world? How confident, resilient, and motivated are we to act when our circumstances are troubled, or when those around us suffer? Has our education helped us to face the challenges of life and death intelligently and to love our fellow human and non-human beings with whom we share this planet? Can any of us say that through education we have understood how our actions form society and, therefore, have the insights that will transform it for the better?

We are born with sharp senses, attentive dispositions, curiosity, interest, and a load of biological faculties innate to learning; however, there is something in the way that we are raised and educated that seems to interfere with the natural flow and individual pace of cognitive development and emotional maturing. So many adults later in life feel incapable of learning something new and thus unable to adapt confidently to changing circumstances. The perpetual modification of methods and techniques continues to promise improved 'solutions' to learning but falls short in many ways, as we are imparted information that is often not relevant to our circumstances and which aims to fulfil a restricted purpose of ephemeral test achievements or securing a career that will potentially fund our desires and fancies. When people judge the 'success' of someone, Money, Influence and Popularity are often the dominant criteria for the assessment. Aren't most of us trying to achieve at least one of these outcomes or waste our lives in admiration of those who have achieved them? It's a conditioning that goes very deep, perpetuated by propaganda and grimly interfering with the development of far more important qualities needed in the world.

Rather than awakening a feeling of care for the planet and

its wider issues, our education missions continue to create environments that prepare children to live an ambitious and notable life. This sounds reasonable until the 'good' intentions result in adults carrying with them a toolbox of knowledge and skills as ammunition to maintain and defend their individual niches amidst a divided society. And so, while ambition and striving are pervasively promoted in our institutions of learning, education remains stagnant and dangerous within its conventional models, or all-too limited within the well-meaning and innovative progressive exceptions.

Division is rife in so many aspects of life. We see it blatantly in the governing structures of our nations as one political party battles against another. We see it in the identification with one's nationality, religion, and political standpoints, or one's gender, class and status. It is evident in the way opinions are debated and comments are posted on social media platforms in response to contentious issues, with people ranting and slinging insults at each other for thinking differently from themselves. It is apparent among professionals in competent fields, where free-thinking experts are unnecessarily discredited for being cautious and questioning the common view. It is happening in our educational settings, big and small, when there is a lack of transparency and dialogue.

The use of the terms and concept of 'us' versus 'them' and 'me' versus 'you' is another expression of separation, and thus a breeding-ground for divisive actions which can plague the workplace, the neighbourhood, and even the home, as people fall out or are shunned for raising a different perspective. We find ourselves unable to fully relate with even our closest friends and family members with a respectful, caring sense of everyone's complex and mixed bag of traits and faculties that have the potential to shift and evolve. Instead, we relate to the images we have formed of them and the categories in which we have pigeonholed them, thus reducing our relationships to something intellectually fabricated. A well-versed, politically active friend shared with me how her knowledge has granted her the tendency to quickly spot the political leanings of the people she meets, thus, if she is not careful, colouring her interactions with them. That innocent openness of youth to unbiased relationships can slowly erode if we are not alert to the limitations of received knowledge and the ways it can influence us.

So much harm has already been done within educational settings. Children and adults have been wounded and traumatised or otherwise warped by the restrictive and coercive environments they are raised in or privy to, thus shaping their future in detrimental ways. Many of us escape into satisfying our pleasures and addictions while consuming, polluting, hurting others and ourselves. Others end up serving the military as trained killing-machines or joining groups or industries which exploit and oppress. Education has not helped us to grow more attentive to the destructive nature of our actions when instead of questioning ourselves and those around us we worship pleasure and authority with its seductions and demands.

I'm sure many of us know of children who have refused to go to school, sobbing with fear or abandonment but who are persuaded to cope until they have a stiff upper lip. Or who have protested about the injustices of actions from adults with their manipulative, nonsensical rules and persistent control. We have seen children start out in life with an innocent, free-thinking and free-feeling direct response to life, but then become 'teacher-pleasers' or dejected souls who are submissive and fearful of being on the 'naughty' list, shamed through reward charts, deprived of play, isolated, and all the other many strategies by which they are coerced to behave, perform, or simply conform.

So, if we feel the significance of these elements, of the multiple connections between held values and world crisis, between personal relationships and war, between daily living and environmental disaster, how are we to make all this more relevant to the Education of our children and of ourselves?

A child does not enter this world racist, divided, caste- and class-conscious, violent or separative. And we don't need to mould and shape the child to perform, conform or compete. What if, instead, we were to engage all bodies while nurturing nobodies: alive, diverse, curious beings who remain liberated from the sense of wanting power, or wanting to compete against others, wanting to stand out for the sake of being noticed, admired, congratulated, or driven to be the best at the expense of others? Without the psychologically crippling effects of comparison that breeds envy, we are then all free to relate as equals.

*Getting bitten by a falling earwig from an oak tree's branches and the
Oak Barn; the decking and seeing its construction*

· 17 ·

In Other Woods

Three years have passed since I last opened that back door, walked to the bottom of that garden and along the track to the sheep field where an array of 'school' goers was to be found, waiting for the 'walking bus' to Inwoods. Energetic girls and boys with their parents or carers, staff and teachers; a flotsam and jetsam of everything it is to be human gathered under the great old oak tree, all with at least one thing in common: a resolve to join forces and be part of another 'wood'.

Another kind of learning and living. Not that we all had the same kind in mind. Not that we were all participating with the exact same intentions or in the same spirit. That would be a lie (and perhaps a disaster). But we had all dropped the idea that conventional schooling with its competitively measurable path of accumulative learning, was the best way to raise the young. We had all decided to take the path less travelled by, or more accurately, ignore any particular 'path' and together try to build a place where learning and living are not separate, and a compassionate future lies in the now.

If I am honest, my sabbatical writing months have left me feeling somewhat nostalgic of those unassuming yet vivacious days among honest kids, demanding parents (in the best sense of that word) and probing educators daring to expose their colours. It was a mostly safe space, a challenging place, somewhat rudimentary but also with substance due to the tireless emphasis on building relationships. This I see is the essence of a learning community, and one that can start with very little. In fact, the less the better. Because when we are free of ideals, conclusions of 'shoulds and should-nots', and without long term projections that might surreptitiously take us on all too common, dangerous trodden paths, we are more likely to learn and act intelligently in response to our real and immediate circumstances.

I appreciated the earnestness within our mud-trodden woodland glade, in which tough blades of grass transformed its winter scene into a green carpet sprinkled with children doing playful, serious, and silly things. This earnestness for a more meaningful education needn't be frantic and worrisome. On the contrary, a slower, gentler pace allows for the kind of leisure where depth and breadth of understanding can permeate our hearts and nourish our minds. It's an earnestness not driven by personal ambition but in the context of finding out who we are, how we relate to one another, and what implications this has for the wider world.

This 'other wood' was not a perfect place, I hasten to remind. There were thorny places to tread and damper conditions to tolerate and accept. The diversity of characters and urge to get involved brought with it the full range of seasons in which a 'sunny' joyful day could cloud over and have us worrying what reactions and unpleasantries would rain instead on our shoulders. But those discomforts were part and parcel of the journey, and, I believe, helped us to grow stronger and a little wiser, and to see that there is still so much inner work to do.

Education is a mutual task. This is a phrase I almost used for the title of this book because education is not the predominant responsibility of policy makers or politicians or directors or teachers. Nor, at the end of the day (when things are not going to the school's plans) should the onus be on parents. We cannot expect education to fundamentally change if we point our blaming fingers at each other and thus reduce the responsibility to a few limited but influential minds and restrictive spaces. If we recognise that the home environment, the neighbourhood, the school or learning centre, and the traits and terrains of one's locality can all inspire the growth of a person, then we can factor this into our daily conversations and planning with all those directly or indirectly involved. Inviting others to join this important work of raising an intelligent child to live in this world with sensitivity and care, makes for a richer landscape of learning for all.

And that landscape must include daily connection with the natural surroundings. Here, I have no qualms about being prescriptive. Aside from the fact that, in retrospect, it was probably the driving force that got me up in the morning, regular contact with nature now – when technology is luring us into virtual worlds from the convenience of our seats – is what will keep our young alive and alert. It is where their senses will be stimulated to see beauty, smell the seasons, feel the temperatures of life; the universal cycles of birth and death with their joys and pains. This is where sensitivity is nurtured and where the greater potential lies to experience in our hearts the non divisive world free of human borders. It is a world that we will want to create if we have a deep connection and respect for nature's ebb and flow.

What else got me up in the morning? Undeniably it was the children (sorry parents!). And in particular, it was the children's boundless energy and frank expression of their encounters with all manner of incidents surrounding them. It was their capacity to feel deeply, to protest loudly, to respond honestly and then to listen astutely if what we offered made sane sense. Yes, I was kept on my toes by their demands and egos, often mirroring my own, but this brought us to an equal place, together with that sense of self that can move one in fabulous or detrimental ways. That 'self', that is either narrow and disconnected or all-embracing and full with 'wholeness', is where I am intrigued to meet the young ones. It is where something of greater understanding lies, and where the delightful child-lived moments of wonder and joy are given like a gift to a dulling adult mind.

Remember that first smile of a baby, those piercing unbiased stares, their delight as toddlers when they touch snow for the first time, and their sudden mastery of phrases that takes us by surprise. I have been bowled over at times by a youngster's wise and unpredictable reflections and their humour that has roused me out of my navel-gazing inertia. Those passionate embraces and little love notes, and sincere tenderness for a baby animal or injured butterfly, stirring one to tears. Here is an opportunity to learn from these developing, playful, less conditioned minds and to be shaken out of our mediocrity. And then, in return, to nurture that great attention to life that is more likely to transform society than any university degree or book full of facts or ideas. Communion and cooperation as a human family can use *self*-knowledge to transform *factual* knowledge into compassionate action for the local and the global.

Who will set out to take good care of the children? How will we ensure that they don't end up following in the footsteps of harm? When will we find out that we are far from alone in the inherited prison of our thinking, and that there is so much potential to learn from each other, both adults and children? These 'other woods', of all shades and sorts, are where together we must humbly go, putting in place the makings of an education where learning takes on a greater meaning.

Afterword

While this work has made reference to the evolution of a school with mention of dates and events, it does not aim to present a complete historical account. Instead, the author has depicted a selection of actual events from when she was in service to this place as truthfully as recollection permits, drawing on past notes, correspondence, as well as questions and feedback from former colleagues and parents. All individuals mentioned in this work are real people; however, to respect their privacy, names have been changed unless explicit consent was given. Lastly, it is important to note that the author's depictions of the school are not indicative of its current operations.

Acknowledgments

It takes a village to raise a child, and a life of joys and pains, and many special relationships to write a book.

I would like to first and foremost thank all my family members, to whom my love can never be expressed enough. To my two sons in particular, who have taught me that parenthood is the most important occupation on the planet. When I receive their love (despite my blunders) it makes me feel as if I can move mountains. To my scary and brilliant big sister, Michaela, who was the first to read half of the work and say, "You have definitely got a book here" (now *that* was scary!). I would like to thank my enthusiastic mum, who in a few words (uncharacteristically) uncovered every hidden concern I had with the last chapter and then inspired me to write one more, just as my words were running dry. Last but not least in the family circle, I am deeply grateful to my lifelong partner, Loic, who remains solidly by my side as I breathe, dream, and obsessively tap away at the keyboard, burning his patient ears with my philosophical chatter while he gets me through life with his unrelenting humour.

I appreciate all those who read or partly read the manuscript at different stages of its evolution and gave me valuable feedback (you know who you are). I'm particularly beholden to Jez Quinton for his detailed comments from the perspective of a colleague and father, thus reassuring me that I wasn't off the mark with my anecdotes and viewpoints. Thank you to Sonya Smith and Anita Sullivan, for their expert advice as published authors when I was halfway through the work and needing some professional encouragement. A heartfelt thank you to Adrian Sydenham for his thorough line edit and insightful suggestions. And to David Skitt for giving it the final careful eye, resulting in precise handwritten edit notes arriving in the mailbox at the end of the drive (frankly, who needs Google Drive!). Finally, my last few words in this section are for my dear friend Lorenzo, who, after sending him the first chapter, nudged me for another one, then another, until seventeen had been pondered and meticulously considered for sense and substance "sense *and* substance? Why both words?" I can hear him ask).

Thank you to dear Abigail Svarovska for her beautiful illustrations and captions, and to the other grown-up children who contributed with their reflections. To the parents who I interviewed and then gave me the freedom to write about their families. A special thank you to all my colleagues who kept their strong shoulders to the Inwoods' wheel for many solid years so that I could also push it forward (and then write about the experience). Parents and children: An enormous thank you to you all for showing me that the next most important (and difficult) occupation on this fragile earth is being an 'educator', and that being honest, working *'with'* rather than *'for'*, is what makes a place dynamic.

This book is printed on paper from sustainable sources managed under the Forest Stewardship Council (FSC) scheme.

It has been printed in the UK to reduce transportation miles and their impact upon the environment.

For every new title that Troubador publishes, we plant a tree to offset CO_2, partnering with the More Trees scheme.

MORE TREES
LET'S PLANT A BILLION TREES

For more about how Troubador offsets its environmental impact, see www.troubador.co.uk/sustainability-and-community